NOTE ON THE FRONTISPIECE

The Frontispiece represents the Fathers of Confederation as assembled at Quebec in 1864. The original picture, painted by the late Mr. Robert Harris, C.M.G., in 1883-1885, hung in the Railway Committee Room of the House of Commons until the Great Fire on February 3, 1916, when unfortunately it was destroyed. Mr. Harris had, however, in his possession a charcoal drawing made as a study for the painting; and after the fire this drawing was acquired by the Dominion Government. From this charcoal drawing the Frontispiece has been reproduced. The portraits are considered to be equal, if not in some cases superior, to those of the painting. For key to portraits see page 7.

The Fathers of Confederation

(For Key see page 7)

H.M.
QUEEN VICTORIA
1867

H.M.
KING GEORGE V
1927

DIAMOND JUBILEE
of the

CONFEDERATION OF CANADA

▽

SIXTY YEARS

OF

CANADIAN

PROGRESS

1867 ⋅ 1927

▽

H.E.
VISCOUNT
MONCK
1867

H.E.
VISCOUNT
WILLINGDON
1927

CONTENTS

LIST OF ILLUSTRATIONS AND DIAGRAMS

FOREWORD

On July 1, 1927, Canada will celebrate the Diamond Jubilee of Confederation and of her birth as a Dominion. Arrangements for the fit and proper observance of this important national event are nearing completion in all parts of the country. Few nations in the world's history have achieved so much of progress in so short a period of time. The occasion is one when all Canadians may well be animated by a just pride in the past and a buoyant confidence in the future.

Among the various steps taken to stimulate interest and to direct and organize opinion and action in this connection, the most notable has been the incorporation, by Act of the Dominion Parliament, of a large and representative body known as "the National Committee for the Celebration of the Diamond Jubilee of Confederation". This Committee has at its head Their Excellencies the Governor-General of Canada and the Viscountess Willingdon; and the membership includes the Lieutenant-Governors and Premiers of the several provinces, the Speakers of the House of Commons and of the Senate, certain members of the Senate and of the House of Commons, and many other representative citizens. It is the general duty of this Committee to organize, in co-operation with the several provinces and with other bodies, an effective celebration of the sixtieth anniversary of the formation of the Dominion. As stated by the Prime Minister when introducing the Bill in the House of Commons, the Committee will seek to co-ordinate the efforts of provinces and municipalities from one end of the Dominion to the other, with those of the Dominion Government.

Later, on the closing day of the first session of the Sixteenth Parliament (April 14, 1927), the following resolution was unanimously passed in the House of Commons and in the Senate:—

"Resolved, that as Canada is approaching the sixtieth anniversary of her founding as a Dominion, the Parliament of Canada place on record its deep appreciation of the achievements of the Fathers of Confederation, and with united voice express its faith and confidence in the future of this our country, and its development as a member of the British Commonwealth of Nations, owing allegiance to His Majesty the King.

"It is the earnest wish of Parliament that the Diamond Jubilee Celebration for which plans are now being rapidly matured, shall commemorate appropriately and enthusiastically the accomplishment of Confederation and the subsequent progress of the Dominion. We trust that this commemoration will lend added inspiration to the patriotic fervour of our people, and afford a clearer vision of our aspirations and ideals, to the end that from sea to sea there may be developed a robust Canadian spirit, and in all things Canadian profounder national unity."

It is in association with this general effort and for a specific purpose that the present handbook has been prepared, by instruction, in the Dominion Bureau of Statistics, and is now being distributed to the people of Canada. Our country is so far-flung, its resources are so multiform, and its achievements have been so many and so varied that, notwithstanding general familiarity with a subject which lies so close to the heart and experience of all, a summary like the present will, it is thought, fulfil a useful purpose in connection with that general appraisement of our progress and present position which is appropriate to the occasion. In particular, the book will be convenient and suggestive for public speakers, teachers, and others who may take a leading part in the celebration, as presenting in readily accessible form the more salient facts of our national progress; so that the minds of the citizens, and especially of the younger generation, may be better attuned to what should be the spirit of the day—a due appreciation of the great tradition and heritage committed to our charge.

The handbook is being distributed by the Bureau to the Legislatures, the press, the municipalities, service clubs, and other institutions of the country, while the National Committee for the Celebration of the Diamond Jubilee is distributing it to the schools and the clergy. Applications for additional copies may be directed to the National Committee, Ottawa.

JAMES MALCOLM,
Minister of Trade and Commerce.

OTTAWA, CANADA,
VICTORIA DAY, 1927.

CHAPTER I.—OUTLINE OF THE POLITICAL HISTORY AND CONFEDERATION OF CANADA

Early History. The French Period.—Canadian recorded history commenced with the discovery of the eastern coast by John Cabot in 1497. Jacques Cartier's voyages (1534-1541) resulted in the exploration of the St. Lawrence as far as Montreal, but Samuel de Champlain was the real founder of Canada, as he was associated with de Monts in establishing Port Royal in 1605 and himself founded Quebec in 1608 and also carried on extensive explorations. Throughout his life Champlain was associated with one or other of the monopolistic trading companies of the period, (trading being the original mainstay of colonization), and for his last eight years he had much to do with the activities of the Company of the Hundred Associates, whose charter, granted in 1627, was cancelled in 1663, when Canada came under the immediate government of the King of France, with a local administration consisting of Governor, Bishop and Intendant, the last-named of whom we might call a business manager. There was also a Sovereign Council to assist the Governor, but it was purely of an advisory character. This system of government, known as Royal Government, lasted until the end of the French

Jacques Cartier

Champlain

1

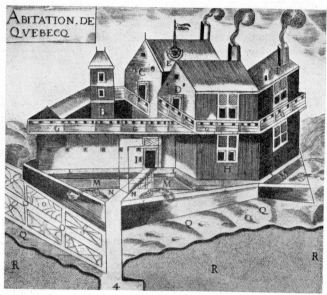

Champlain's "Abitation" at Quebec

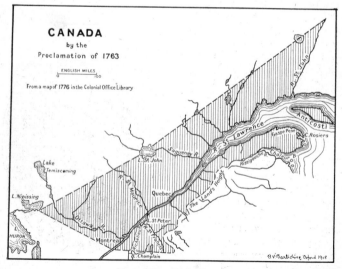

Map of Canada in 1763

period in 1760. Among the various governors, the name of Frontenac is outstanding, among the Bishops, Laval, and among the Intendants, Talon. In a recapitulation like the present, however, devoted solely to forms of government, it is impossible even to suggest, much less fill in, the romantic and picturesque background of the French *régime* in Canada—that succession of stirring incidents clustered about such names as Maisonneuve and La Mère de l'Incarnation, Dollard, D'Iberville and La Vérendrye, Marquette and La Salle, which opened up what is now the Dominion to the knowledge of the civilized world and persists to-day in some of our most notable institutions.

General Wolfe

Nova Scotia or Acadia had already been surrendered to the British by the Treaty of Utrecht in 1713, while the Seven Years' War saw the great struggle for the St. Lawrence valley between Wolfe and Montcalm—a struggle which cost both leaders their lives at the battle of the Plains of Abraham.

The British Period.—Canada, including Cape Breton island and what is now New Brunswick, became after the Treaty of Paris in 1763 a British crown colony with limits as shown on the map opposite. For several years thereafter the government was of a purely military character.

In 1774, when the American Revolution was visibly approaching, the boundaries of the prov-

General Montcalm

ince of Canada were extended by the Quebec Act south to the Ohio river and west to the Mississippi. It also established a council with limited powers, sanctioned the use of French law in civil matters, and granted full freedom for the exercise of the Roman Catholic religion. After the war, in which Canada was saved for the British flag by the energy of Sir Guy Carleton, then Governor, who with the co-operation of the better elements of the population repulsed the attacks of Montgomery and Arnold, the Treaty of Versailles surrendered the fertile but unpeopled territory south of the Great Lakes to the United States. Thereafter the coming of the United Empire Loyalists reinforced the English-speaking population of Nova Scotia and peopled New Brunswick and Ontario.

The Constitutional Act of 1791 divided the English-speaking province of Ontario or Upper Canada from the mainly French-speaking province of Lower Canada or Quebec and gave to each Representative Government, which had existed in Nova Scotia since 1758, in Prince Edward Island since 1769 (first Legislature met, 1773), and in New Brunswick since 1784 (first Legislature met, 1786). The British North American provinces, as they existed at the end of the eighteenth century, are shown on the map below.

In the early nineteenth century, there took place the war of 1812-15 with the United States, in which Sir Isaac Brock and Colonel de Salaberry were outstanding figures in the defence of Canada, which, though fighting against heavy odds, lost not an acre of territory by the Treaty of Ghent at the close of the war.

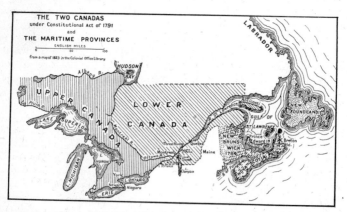

Map of The Two Canadas and the Maritimes, 1791

4

The Representative Government granted in 1791, however, while it gave the representatives of the people a considerable voice in the administration, went only part way in the direction of popular government and resulted in bitter quarrels between the Legislative Assemblies and the Governors—quarrels which, as the Legislative Assemblies secured increasing control of the finances, could end in only one way. These quarrels finally led in Upper and Lower Canada to the abortive rebellions of 1837-38, which, however, brought about the sending of Lord Durham to Canada, the union of the two

Sir Guy Carleton
(Lord Dorchester)

provinces and the decision to grant Responsible Government. During the first seven years of the Union, the meaning and scope of Responsible Government were hotly debated, but after the formation of the Lafontaine-Baldwin government in 1848 it was definitely recognized that the Governor, like the King, did not govern, but the Government was entrusted to whichever of the political leaders of the moment could command the support of the majority in the Legislative Assembly. In the same year, 1848, when Lord Elgin was Governor-General, Responsible Government was given to Nova Scotia and New Brunswick, and in 1851 to Prince Edward Island.

Meanwhile, far out on the Pacific coast, a new settlement was being established on Vancouver island, where coal had been discovered in 1849, but to which the fur-trade had penetrated both by land and sea long before—Sir Alexander Mackenzie's heroic exploit in crossing the continent having taken place in 1793. Representative Government was conceded to this Colony in 1856. A little later the discovery of gold on the mainland led to a great rush of miners, and the mainland was constituted a separate colony in 1858. In 1864 a Legislative Council was established in which some of the members were appointed by the Governor and others elected. Two years later the provinces of British Columbia and Vancouver Island were united and the first Legislative Council of British Columbia met, being partly nominated and partly elected. In 1871, just prior to the entry of British Columbia into Confederation, this Council passed the Constitution Act, providing for a Legislative Assembly of 25 members, to be substituted for the Council itself. This Act came into force July 19, 1871.

The Confederation Movement.—The project of uniting the British North American colonies was adumbrated as early as 1789 by William Smith, a former Chief Justice of Canada, whose plan included a nominated council and an assembly elected by the members of the provincial assemblies. Twenty-five years later, another Chief Justice (Sewell) proposed a somewhat similar scheme. In the absence of rapid communication and transportation, however, no real union was possible.

With the introduction of railways and telegraphs the idea of Confederation came within the range of practical politics. In 1850 the British American League stated in its prospectus that the true solution of the difficulties of the time lay in the Confederation of all the provinces, and in 1851 the Hon. Henry Sherwood, who had been Attorney-General for Upper Canada and Prime Minister, published a plan for the federative union of the British North American provinces, providing for two elective chambers and a system of local Legislatures, somewhat similar to those existing to-day, except that the Provincial Governors were to be elected.

In 1858 Alexander Galt, member for Sherbrooke in the Canadian Legislative Assembly, advocated both in and out of parliament the confederation of all the British North American provinces, but although he was successful in inducing the Cartier-Macdonald Government, of which he was a member, to send a mission to England to discuss the matter with the Imperial authorities, nothing tangible resulted. It was really the deadlock in the Canadian Legislative Assembly that some years later induced the Government of Canada to take the matter up. A second cause was the notice given by the United States, that the reciprocity treaty would be abrogated, thus forcing Canada to look for new channels of trade. A third was the intimation from the British Government that Canada must, to a large extent, provide for its own defence. These things made Confederation a practical instead of an academic question. In 1864 a Coalition Government was formed in Canada for the purpose of negotiating the confederation of the British North American provinces, failing which, they undertook to apply the federal principle as between Upper and Lower Canada. This Coalition Government, of which Sir Etienne Taché was the head, included John A. Macdonald and George Etienne Cartier, together with George Brown, Oliver Mowat and William McDougall as representatives of the opposition.

Meanwhile a somewhat similar movement was taking shape in the Maritime Provinces, where there were three Governments and three Legislatures in an area far smaller than either Upper or Lower Canada. The Legislatures of the three provinces authorized their Governments to hold a joint conference to discuss the expediency of a

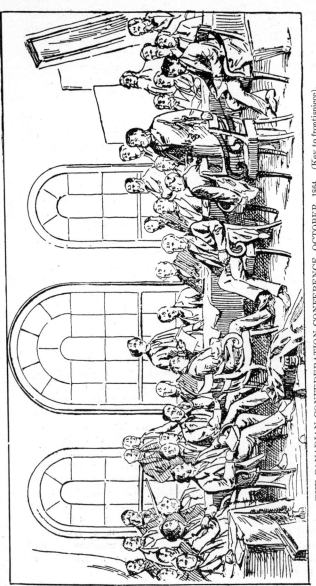

THE CANADIAN CONFEDERATION CONFERENCE, OCTOBER, 1864. (Key to frontispiece).

1. Major Barnard. 2. W. H. Steeves. 3. E. Whelan. 4. W. A. Henry. 5. C. Fisher. 6. J. H. Gray. 7. E. Palmer. 8. G. Coles. 9. F. B. T. Carter. 10. J. C. Chapais. 11. S. L. Tilley. 12. A. Shea. 13. E. B. Chandler. 14. A. Campbell. 15. A. G. Archibald. 16. H. Langevin. 17. J. A. Macdonald. 18. G. E. Cartier. 19. E. P. Taché. 20. Geo. Brown. 21. T. H. Haviland. 22. A. T. Galt. 23. P. Mitchell. 24. O. Mowat. 25. J. Cockburn. 26. R. B. Dickey. 27. C. Tupper. 28. J. H. Gray. 29. W. H. Pope. 30. W. McDougall. 31. T. D'Arcy McGee. 32. A. A. Macdonald. 33. J. McCully. 34. J. M. Johnson.

union of the three provinces under one Government and Legislature, and this conference met at Charlottetown on September 1, 1864. The Canadian Government, having learned of this conference, asked for and received permission for its delegates to attend and present their point of view. They did so and prevailed upon the representatives of the Maritime Provinces to adjourn their conference and meet at Quebec to discuss the *federal union* of all the provinces rather than the *legislative union* of the Maritime provinces only. At this second conference Newfoundland, as well as Canada and the Maritime Provinces, was represented. The Quebec conference met on October 10, 1864, and continued until October 29. The resolutions which it accepted were later on incorporated in the British North America Act. These resolutions, 72 in number, were laid before the Legislature of Canada at the following session and approved by a vote of 91 to 33. In the Maritime Provinces, however, the reception which the resolutions received was not so favourable. In New Brunswick the confederation policy of Mr. Tilley was defeated in a general election and in Nova Scotia the opposition was so strong that Dr. Tupper, the leader of the Government, fell back on the original proposal of the Maritime union. However, the situation gradually improved, and on April 17, 1866, the Nova Scotia Assembly, by a vote of 31 to 19, authorized the appointment of delegates to arrange with the Imperial Government a scheme of union which would safeguard the rights and interests of the province. After another general election in New Brunswick a similar resolution was passed there on June 30, 1866, by a vote of 31 to 8. The delegates of Canada, of Nova Scotia and New Brunswick met at the Westminster Palace Hotel in London on December 4, 1866, Prince Edward Island and Newfoundland not being represented. The resolutions of the Quebec conference were taken up, considered *seriatim*, amended in certain particulars and adopted anew, the amendments granting more favourable financial terms to the Maritime Provinces. The title desired for the new confederation by the conference was the "Kingdom of Canada," but this was disallowed on the ground that the name "Kingdom" might not be acceptable to the people of the United States and the name "Dominion" was substituted. The resolutions, as amended by the London conference, were now passed by the Imperial Parliament as the British North America Act, receiving the Royal Assent on March 29, 1867. On May 22 was issued the Royal proclamation, uniting the provinces of Canada, Nova Scotia and New Brunswick into one Dominion under the name of Canada, and on July 1, 1867, the Dominion commenced to exist. (Certain provisions of the B.N.A. Act are set out in Chap. III and the Act is reprinted as Appendix III.)

Mural Bronze in the Provincial Building, Charlottetown, commemorating the Meeting of September 1, 1864

The Expansion of Canada.—The early years of Confederation under Sir John A. Macdonald as prime minister, were of a somewhat stormy character, owing to the agitation in Nova Scotia for the repeal of the union, and to the North West rebellion of 1870, arising out of the transfer of the enormous territories of the Hudson's Bay Company to the new Dominion. This transfer, however, became effective on July 15, 1870, and Manitoba was admitted into Confederation as the fifth province of the Dominion. On July 20, 1871, British Columbia entered Confederation under an agreement stipulating for the construction of a Canadian Pacific Railway, and Prince Edward Island joined its fortunes with those of the Dominion on July 1, 1873. On September 1, 1880, all British possessions in North America and the adjacent islands, except Newfoundland and its dependencies, were annexed to Canada by Imperial Order of July 31, this Order in Council extending the Dominion of Canada far northward into the Arctic regions. In 1895 negotiations for the inclusion of Newfoundland in the Confederation proved abortive and Newfoundland still remains a separate government. In September, 1905, about the middle of the long premiership of Sir Wilfrid Laurier, the new provinces of Alberta and Saskatchewan were formed from the old Hudson Bay territory and in 1912 the boundaries of Manitoba, Ontario and Quebec were extended northward to Hudson Strait and Hudson Bay, James Bay and the 60th parallel of latitude. Canada, north of the 60th parallel, has been formed for administrative purposes into the territories of Yukon, Mackenzie, Keewatin and Franklin, the latter including the islands of the Arctic Ocean.

The evolution of governmental machinery and finance which accompanied the above expansion is briefly treated in Chapter III, while a chronology of Confederated Canada will be found as Appendix I.

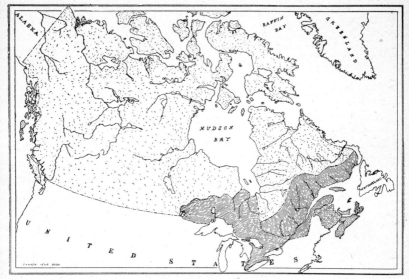

Map of Canada in 1867

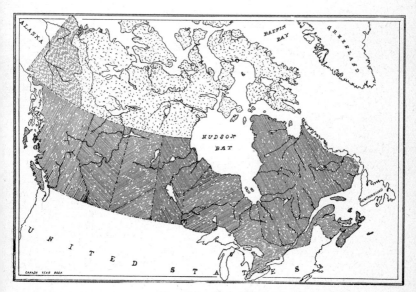

Map of Canada in 1927

CHAPTER II.—AREA—NATURAL RESOURCES—CLIMATE

Area

In the sixty years since Confederation, the area of the Dominion of Canada has been greatly enlarged in the manner described at the close of Chapter I.

The four original provinces contained 350,188 square miles of land and inland waters, of which the original land area was 338,224 square miles. In 1881, after purchase of the vast Hudson Bay Territory in 1870 and the admission of British Columbia in 1871 and of Prince Edward Island in 1873, the area of the Dominion is stated in the Census of 1881 as 3,470,392 square miles. Since that time, further exploration in the northern regions has resulted in increasing the estimated land area of Canada to 3,654,200 square miles, which, together with a water area of 142,923 square miles, gives a grand total of 3,797,123[1] square miles, or well over ten times the area of the Dominion as originally constituted. The details of this growth are given in the following table:—

Land Area of the Dominion (sq. miles) in 1867, etc., and in 1927

Province	Date of organization or admission	At organization or admission	In 1927
Original Confederation—			
Ontario	July 1, 1867	101,715	365,880
Quebec	" 1, 1867	187,530	690,865
New Brunswick	" 1, 1867	27,911	27,911
Nova Scotia	" 1, 1867	21,068	21,068
Admitted—			
British Columbia	July 20, 1871	353,416	353,416
Prince Edward Island	" 1, 1873	2,184	2,184
Organized—			
Manitoba	July 15, 1870	13,965	231,926
Saskatchewan	Sept. 1, 1905	243,381	243,381
Alberta	" 1, 1905	252,925	252,925
Territories		2,450,998[1]	1,464,644

Natural Resources

It follows from the above that the natural resources of Canada are those of a continent rather than of a country; nowhere else in the world have the same number of people such enormous undeveloped natural resources at their disposal. This fact is mainly responsible for

[1] This area has been reduced by perhaps 100,000 square miles as a result of the recent decision of the Judicial Committee of the Privy Council in the Labrador boundary question.

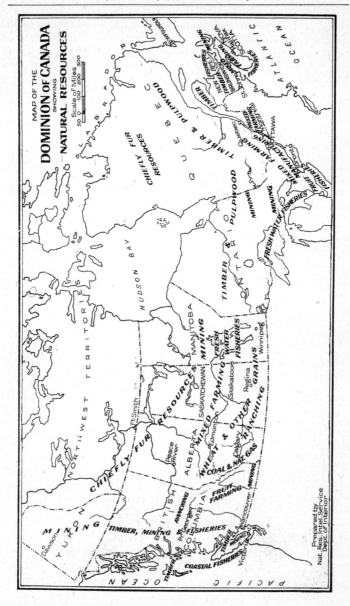

the heavy investments in Canada of British and United States capital (probably $5,250 millions in all), in addition to the rapidly growing capital of the people of Canada itself.

The natural resources of Canada consist mainly of agricultural lands, forests, fisheries, minerals, waterpowers, and fur-bearing animals. Though the later chapters of this booklet deal with their development incidentally, they may be recapitulated in summary form below:—

Agricultural Lands.—The breeding of new early-ripening varieties of grain, such as Garnet wheat, is materially increasing the area capable of agricultural development, so that the agricultural possibilities of the lands north of the 60th parallel are as yet practically unknown. Apart from these considerations, it is estimated that out of the 1,401,316,413 acres of the land area of the nine provinces, approximately 358,162,190 acres are available for use in agricultural production, being 2½ times the present occupied area and 5 times the present improved area of farm lands. In all the provinces except Prince Edward Island large areas are still available for settlement and, while the nature of the soil and of the climate varies, generally speaking grain, root and fodder crops can be profitably grown in all the provinces, while stock-raising is successfully carried on both in the more densely settled areas and on their frontiers.

The Maritime Provinces are noted for their fruit and vegetable crops, perhaps particularly for the oat and potato crops of Prince Edward Island and New Brunswick and the apples of the Annapolis valley in Nova Scotia. Quebec and Ontario are pre-eminently mixed

Wheat Harvested at Fort Vermilion, 350 miles north of Edmonton
Photo by Can. Govt. Motion Picture Bureau

farming communities, various districts specializing in dairying, tobacco, sheep, etc., while the Niagara peninsula in Ontario has long been famous for its fruit crops of both large and small varieties. In Manitoba, Saskatchewan and Alberta, the production of grain is still of primary importance but is giving way to more diversified types of agriculture, while the stock-raising industry, once so typical of the western prairies, is regaining much of its former importance. In British Columbia the fertile valleys are devoted principally to apple and other fruit crops, and numerous districts along the coast and on Vancouver island are devoted to general farming and market gardening.

Of the larger areas of land still available for settlement, the clay belt of northern Ontario and Quebec, in which splendid crops are grown, is to a large extent undeveloped, as well as an even larger area in northern Saskatchewan and Alberta.

Forests.—Canada's forest areas are:—(1) the great coniferous forest of the Rocky Mountains and Pacific Coast; (2) the northern forest, stretching in a wide curve from the Yukon north of the Great Lakes to Labrador; and (3) the forest extending from Lake Huron through southern Ontario and Quebec to New Brunswick and the Atlantic Coast. Altogether the timber lands of the Dominion are estimated at 1,227,000 square miles, some of which is agricultural land. This area is estimated to contain 482,075,000,000 feet board measure of saw timber and 1,279,705,000 cords of pulpwood, cordwood, poles, etc., making a total equivalent to 246,826,000,000 cubic feet.

Vegetables Grown at Fort Vermilion, 350 miles north of Edmonton
Photo by Can. Govt. Motion Picture Bureau

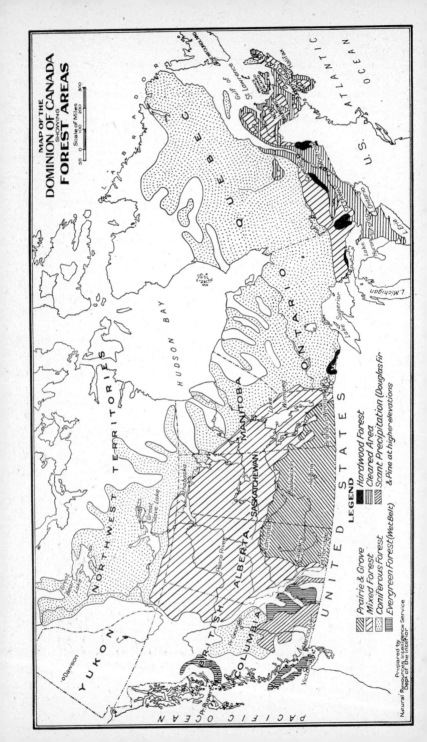

These figures place Canada next to the United States among the countries of the world with respect to forest resources.

Fisheries.—Fisheries were the first of Canadian resources to be exploited by Europeans. Canada's Atlantic fishing grounds extend along a coast line of more than 5,000 miles and cover an area of not less than 200,000 square miles of pure cold sea water coming down from the Arctic region and containing an immense quantity of fish of the

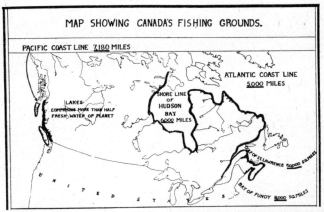

MAP SHOWING CANADA'S FISHING GROUNDS.

Atlantic Waters—4/5 of the North Atlantic fishing grounds or 200,000 sq.
  miles. Inshore waters on the Atlantic seaboard 15,000 sq. miles.
Inland waters (half the fresh water on the planet) 140,000 sq. miles.
Estuarian fisheries of British Columbia and Pacific Ocean fisheries.

highest food value, including cod, halibut, haddock, herring and mackerel, while the inshore fisheries number the lobster, oyster, salmon, gaspereau, smelt, trout and maskinonge. Other fishing grounds include the inshore expanses of the St. Lawrence River, the Great Lakes (whitefish, trout and herring), Hudson Bay, with a shore line of 6,000 miles, and the Pacific Coast, with its shore line of 7,000 miles and with its estuarian salmon fisheries making up two-fifths of the fish products of the Dominion.

Minerals.—The numerous and varied mineral deposits of Canada constitute another of her most important resources, and Canada is now becoming one of the leading mining countries of the world, though her mineral resources are still but imperfectly known. With regard to coal it is estimated that the reserves available amount to 1,234,269 million metric tons or about one-sixth of the total reserves of the world; 85 per cent of these are in Alberta. Extensive oil fields exist in the western provinces and some smaller oil fields in Ontario have been exploited. In the production of natural gas Canada comes second among the countries of the world. In nickel and asbestos again Canada possesses by far the greater part of the reserves of the world, while in gold she is now the third country in production, and looks forward to passing the United States.

Water-Powers.—Canada's water area of 142,923 square miles, distributed throughout all parts of the country, provides a large amount of potential electric energy. It is estimated that 18,255,316 h.p. are available at a minimum yearly flow, 32,075,998 at ordinary six months flow, and that a turbine installation of 41,700,000 h.p. is possible, the present installation of 4,556,219 h.p. being less than 11 per cent of the possible. These water powers have, up to the present, been chiefly used in the pulp and paper industry, in mining and in the electro-chemical, electro-metallurgical, and the flour-milling industries. This "white coal" enables the chief manufacturing area of Canada in Ontario and Quebec to "carry on" in the absence of indigenous available supplies of coal.

Furs.—In the northern and unsettled areas of Canada, one of the chief resources is the fur-bearing animals, whose skins are in great and increasing demand. The large uninhabited areas of northern Quebec, Ontario, Manitoba and the North West Territories furnish subsistence for many of the most highly prized fur-bearing animals, such as the beaver, fisher, fox, marten and others. During the year 1924-25 the value of pelts taken from wild animals in Canada was $15,441,564.

Game and Scenery.—Canada's position as one of the least densely settled countries of the English-speaking world alongside of a much more settled area and just across the sea from the densely populated British Isles, combines with the profusion of her game resources and with her scenery to attract great and increasing numbers of sportsmen and tourists to her shores. The valleys of Nova Scotia and New Brunswick, the broken lake country of northern Ontario and Quebec, together with the mountain districts of British Columbia, offer to the hunter and the fisherman a practically inexhaustible game preserve, and to the tourist new types of scenery. In particular, British Columbia is among the most beautiful mountain areas of the world. In order that the natural beauties of the country may be preserved and popularized, the National Parks Branch of the Department of the Interior administers eleven parks, set apart for this purpose, including such great mountain areas as Jasper Park in northern Alberta, and the Rocky Mountain Park, also in Alberta, containing 4,400 and 2,751 square miles respectively, also Kootenay Park, Glacier Park and Yoho

Park in British Columbia. Many Provincial Parks are also maintained. The tourist traffic is annually becoming larger and more valuable to the country.

Cape Trinity, on the Saguenay River
Photo by Can. Govt. Motion Picture Bureau

Climate

It is difficult to generalize concerning the climate of so large an area. The greater part of the Dominion is in what may be called the colder temperate zone, while at the extreme north Arctic conditions prevail, and in certain parts, especially in southern Ontario and in Vancouver island, the products are those of the warmer temperate zone.

In the main, the climate of Canada may be described as "continental", that is, subject to extremes of heat in summer and cold in winter which are not generally felt on islands or on the sea coast in the same latitudes. At the same time a considerable part of Canada is comparatively near the sea or to great bodies of water which have a tendency to modify the climate, as, for example, the Maritime provinces, the peninsula of Southern Ontario and the coast regions of British Columbia (*see* the isothermal lines in the accompanying map).

Roughly, the climate of Canada may be classified under four main types, namely: (1) the valley and coastal type of British Columbia; (2) the Prairie type; (3) Ontario and Quebec; (4) the Maritime provinces.

19

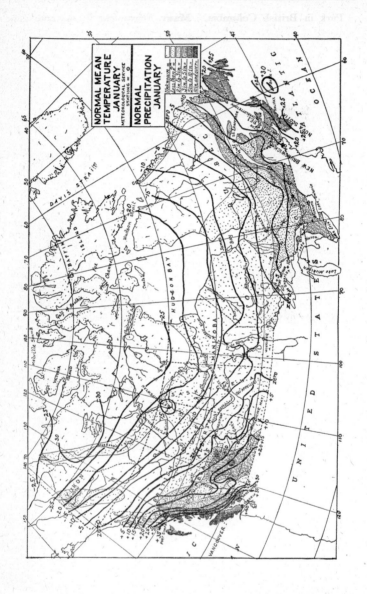

The valley and coastal type of British Columbia is characterized by moderate temperatures in summer and winter and high precipitation on the coast. In the interior valleys of the Okanagan and Kootenay country the winter temperatures are distinctly lower and the precipitation very much less than on the coast.

The outstanding features of the prairie climate are the much scantier precipitation and the more severe cold of winter. Fortunately, the precipitation comes at the time of year when it is most needed, in the growing period, though in southern Alberta the summer precipitation is often deficient. The climate of the Prairie Provinces is also modified by their elevation, which increases steadily as one proceeds west from Winnipeg. Thus, while the Canadian Pacific Railway at Winnipeg station is 766 feet above mean sea level, it is 1,204 feet at Brandon, 1,896 feet at Regina, 2,181 feet at Medicine Hat and 3,437 feet at Calgary. These high elevations are partly responsible for the strong cold winds which are a feature of the prairie climate.

Ontario and Quebec are comparatively mild in the southern districts, but severe in the winter and with a shorter summer in the more northern areas, where also there is a less precipitation. Quebec is generally somewhat colder than Ontario. East of Quebec city the summers are distinctly cool, the normal mean temperature for July being under 65°. Only in the country on the shores of lake Erie, lake Ontario and the St. Lawrence is the normal mean temperature in July over 70°.

In the Maritime provinces the climate is characterized by heavier precipitation than in Ontario, and in the southern districts by more equable temperatures. Nova Scotia has a distinctly warmer winter than New Brunswick. The southwestern part of Nova Scotia is the only part of Eastern Canada where the normal mean temperature in January is above 25°.

The winter sports of Canada, representing the advantage now taken of what was once considered a disagreeable hardship, are annually attracting an increasing number of tourists.

CHAPTER III.

THE CONSTITUTION AND GOVERNMENT OF CANADA—PUBLIC FINANCES (DOMINION, PROVINCIAL AND MUNICIPAL)

The constitutional development of Canada, from the time of its coming under British rule down to Confederation, is mainly based upon four important acts of the British Parliament, the Quebec Act of 1774, the Constitutional Act of 1791, the Act of Union of 1840, and the British North America Act of 1867[1]. The first of these is chiefly important as establishing the French civil law throughout the area then contained in the province of Quebec. The second is noteworthy for the division of the province into the French-speaking province of Lower Canada and the English-speaking province of Upper Canada, and for the concession of representative government through an elective legislative assembly, which, however, had no control over the executive government except in so far as it could refuse to vote taxes (the non-tax revenue of the province was outside of its control). The third of the above-mentioned acts reunited the two Canadas under a single Legislature and conceded the principle of responsible government, the executive administration being henceforth the creature of the Legislature. The fourth separated the two Canadas from their existing legislative union to make them provinces, each administering its own local affairs, in a wider Confederation, which within a comparatively short period so extended its boundaries so as to take in the whole of British North America except Newfoundland and Labrador.

Canada in the Empire and Among the Nations.—Since Confederation there has taken place a gradual development of the powers of the Canadian Government, due in part to a more liberal attitude among British statesmen. Thus, in 1878, the Hon. Edward Blake secured the issuance of a new set of instructions to the Governor General providing that, with unimportant exceptions, he should act upon the advice of his Ministers. A gradual development in the status of the Dominion was also evident at the successive Colonial Conferences, the name of which in 1907 was changed to Imperial Conferences, when also, it was provided that further conferences should be between the Government of the United Kingdom and the Governments of the self-governing Dominions, and that the Prime Minister of the United Kingdom instead of the Colonial Secretary was to be President of the Conference, a move toward recognizing that the British Government was simply *primus inter pares* among the nations of the empire.

---

[1] The B.N.A. Act is reprinted as Appendix III to this publication.

The Victory Memorial Tower, Parliament Buildings, Ottawa

Drawing by N.R.I. Service

The Conference of 1911 met under this arrangement. Later, during the war, was evolved what was known as the Imperial War Conference, a gathering of the five members of the British War Cabinet and the Prime Ministers of the self-governing Dominions. At the close of the war, on the initiative of Sir Robert Borden, then Prime Minister of Canada, the Dominions secured recognition as signatory powers of the Treaty of Versailles and were accepted as members of the League of Nations, since which time a Canadian Minister of the Crown, the Hon. Raoul Dandurand, has acted as President of the Assembly of the League of Nations.

The present position of Canada in the British Commonwealth of Nations was clearly defined at the Imperial Conference of 1926, attended by Rt. Hon. W. L. Mackenzie King, Prime Minister, and Hon. Ernest Lapointe, Minister of Justice, on behalf of Canada. The Report of the Inter-imperial Relations Committee recommended that in future the Governor General should be regarded as the personal representative of the Crown rather than as an official of the Government of Great Britain and that the Dominions might have their own representatives in foreign countries. A Minister to the United States has now been appointed. In defining the relative position of Great

The Speaker's Chair, House of Commons, Ottawa

Photo by Can. Govt. Motion Picture Bureau

Britain and the self-governing Dominions, the Committee made the following statement, which was endorsed by the Conference:—

"They are autonomous Communities within the British Empire, equal in status, in no way subordinate one to another in any aspect of their domestic or external affairs, though united by a common allegiance to the Crown, and freely associated as members of the British Commonwealth of Nations."

The Constitution of Canada

Since the British North America Act, based on the agreement of our own representatives, defines our internal constitution, it and its consequences must be further analyzed under the headings of "Dominion Government" and "Provincial Government."

In the preamble to the Act it is stated that the provinces of Canada, Nova Scotia and New Brunswick "have expressed their desire to be federally united into one Dominion, with a Constitution similar in principle to that of the United Kingdom". Thus our constitution is not an imitation of that of the United States, it is the British Constitution federalized. Like the British and unlike the American Constitution, it is not a written constitution. The many unwritten conventions of the British Constitution are also recognized in our own; what we have in the British North America Act is a written delimitation of the respective powers of the Dominion and Provincial Governments, and an enactment of the terms of the Confederation Agreement.

The Dominion Government.—The British North America Act declares that the executive government of Canada shall continue to be vested in the Sovereign of the United Kingdom (sec. 9), represented for Dominion purposes by the Governor-General, as for provincial purposes by the Lieutenant-Governor. The Governor-General is advised by the King's Privy Council for Canada, a committee of which constitutes the Ministry of the day.

The Dominion Parliament consists of the King, the Senate and the House of Commons. It must meet at least once a year, so that twelve months do not elapse between the last meeting in one session and the first meeting in the next. Senators, 96 in number, who are appointed for life by the Governor General in Council, must be 30 years of age, British subjects, residents of the province for which they are appointed, and possess $4,000 over and above their liabilities. Members of the House of Commons (245 in 1927) are elected by the people for the duration of the Parliament, which may not be longer than five years.

Powers of Parliament.—The Dominion Parliament has exclusive legislative authority in all matters relating to the following: public debt and property; regulation of trade and commerce; raising of money by any mode of taxation; borrowing of money on the public credit; postal service; census and statistics; militia, military and naval service and defence; fixing and providing for salaries and allowances of the officers of the government; beacons, buoys and lighthouses; navigation and shipping; quarantine and the establishment and maintenance of marine hospitals; sea-coast and inland fisheries; ferries on an international or interprovincial frontier; currency and coinage; banking, incorporation of banks, and issue of paper money; savings banks; weights and measures; bills of exchange and promissory notes; interest; legal tender; bankruptcy and insolvency; patents of invention and discovery; copyrights; Indians and lands reserved for Indians; naturalization and aliens; marriage and divorce; the criminal law, except the constitution of courts of criminal jurisdiction, but including the procedure in criminal matters; the establishment, maintenance and management of penitentiaries; such classes of subjects as are expressly excepted in the enumeration of the classes of subjects by the Act exclusively assigned to the legislatures of the Provinces.

Public Finance.—At Confederation the revenues which had previously accrued to the treasuries of the provinces were transferred to the Dominion, notably the customs duties. The public works, cash assets and other property of the provinces, except lands, mines, minerals and royalties, also became Dominion property. In its turn, the Dominion was to become responsible for the debts of the provinces. Since the main source of the revenues of the provinces was now taken over, the Dominion was to pay annual subsidies to the provinces for the support of their governments and legislatures. These subsidies have from time to time been increased.

The Confederation of the provinces occurred at a time when throughout the English-speaking world the doctrine of *laisser faire* was generally accepted, with the consequence that the functions of Government were at their minimum and required a comparatively small expenditure to perform, so that the amount of revenue collected from the taxpayers was comparatively small, and the tax revenue still smaller. The Confederation Agreement, however, provided for completion of the Intercolonial railway, and that with British Columbia for the construction of the Canadian Pacific railway; later on the National Transcontinental was undertaken. Indeed, the single item of railways and canals accounts for almost the entire increase in the national debt down to the Great War, which cost the country some $1,700,000,000 besides the heavy obligations for pensions. Further, the current ideas of the functions of Government differ very widely from those which existed at the time of Confederation. Literally scores of increased services are now required from the Government. Where the Government at Confederation had only about 1,500 employees it has to-day some 39,000.

The growth of the Dominion revenue, the Dominion expenditure, and the net public debt from the first year of Confederation to the present, is briefly outlined in the following table:—

Dominion Finances, 1867-1926

Year	Estimated or census population	Revenue receipts	Total expenditure	Net debt at end of year
	No.	$	$	$
1868	3,372,000	13,687,928	14,071,689	75,757,135
1871	3,485,761	19,335,561	19,293,478	77,706,518
1881	4,324,810	29,635,298	33,796,643	155,395,780
1891	4,833,239	38,579,311	40,793,208	237,809,031
1901	5,371,315	52,514,701	57,982,866	268,480,004
1911	7,206,643	117,780,409	122,861,250	340,042,052
1921	8,788,483	434,386,537[1]	528,302,513[2]	2,340,878,984[3]
1926	9,390,300	380,745,506[1]	355,186,423[2]	2,389,731,099

[1] Exclusive of special receipts of $1,905,648 in 1921 and $2,147,503 in 1926.
[2] Includes advances to railways, Canadian Government Merchant Marine, etc., of $110,662,655 in 1921 and of $11,205,910 in 1926.
[3] The maximum net debt of Canada at the end of any fiscal year was $2,453,776,869 at Mar. 31, 1923.

The Provincial Governments

In each of the provinces the King is represented by a Lieutenant-Governor, appointed by the Governor-General in Council, and governing with the advice and assistance of his Ministry or Executive Council, which is responsible to the Legislature and resigns office when it ceases to enjoy the confidence of that body. The Legislatures are uni-cameral, consisting of a Legislative Assembly elected by the people, except in Quebec and Nova Scotia, where there is a Legislative Council as well as a Legislative Assembly.

Powers of Provincial Legislatures.—The Legislature in each Province may exclusively make laws in relation to the following matters: amendment of the constitution of the Province, except as regards the Lieutenant-Governor; direct taxation within the province; borrowing of money on the credit of the province; establishment and tenure of provincial offices and appointment and payment of provincial officers; the management and sale of public lands belonging to the province and of the timber and wood thereon; the establishment, maintenance and management of public and reformatory prisons in and for the province; the establishment, maintenance and management of hospitals, asylums, charities and eleemosynary institutions in and for the province, other than marine hospitals; municipal institutions in the province; shop, saloon, tavern, auctioneer and other licenses issued for the raising of provincial or municipal revenue; local works and undertakings other than interprovincial or international lines of ships, railways, canals, telegraphs, etc., or works which, though wholly situated within one province, are declared by the Dominion Parliament to be for the general advantage either of Canada or of two or more provinces; the incorporation of companies with provincial objects; the solemnization of marriage in the province; property and civil rights in the province; the administration of justice in the province, including the constitution, maintenance and organization of provincial courts both of civil and criminal jurisdiction, and including procedure in civil matters in these courts; the imposition of punishment by fine, penalty, or imprisonment for enforcing any law of the province relating to any of the aforesaid subjects; generally all matters of a merely local or private nature in the province. Further, in and for each province the Legislature may, under section 93, exclusively make laws in relation to education, subject to certain provisions for the protection of religious minorities, who are to retain the privileges and rights enjoyed before Confederation.

Provincial Public Finance.—Provincial Governments in Canada are in the position, under section 118 of the British North America Act, 1867 (30 and 31 Vict., c. 3), and the British North America Act, 1907 (7 Edw. VII, c. 11), of having a considerable assured income in subsidies from the Dominion treasury. In addition, through their retention of ownership of their lands, minerals and other natural resources, the provinces which, by the voluntary action of their previously existing governments, entered Confederation, raise considerable revenues through land sales, sales of timber, mining royalties, leases of water-powers, etc., while the Prairie Provinces receive from the Dominion special grants in lieu of land revenues. Further, under section 92 of the British North America Act, Provincial Legislatures are given authority to impose direct taxation within the province for provincial purposes and to borrow money on the sole credit of the province.

While the *laisser faire* school of political thought was predominant throughout the country, provincial receipts and expenditures were generally very moderate. From the commencement of the twentieth century, however, the Canadian public, more especially in Ontario and the West, began to demand increased services from the government, particularly in respect of education, sanitation, and the ownership and operation of public utilities. The performance of these functions necessitated increased revenues, which had in the main to be raised by taxation. Among the chief methods of taxation to be employed has been the taxation of corporations and estates. Prominent among the objects of increased expenditure in this same period are education, public buildings, public works, labour protection, charities, hospitals and corrections. Provincial government is cheaper per head in the *laisser faire* eastern provinces, but this is not to be taken

Provincial Parliament Buildings

1. Quebec; 2. Fredericton; 3. Halifax; 4. Charlottetown; 5. Regina; 6. Edmonton; 7. Winnipeg; 8. Victoria; 9. Toronto

Can. Govt. Motion Picture Bureau.

as evidence that the larger services rendered to the public in the western provinces are not worth what is being paid for them.

The expansion in the ordinary revenues and expenditures of the provincial governments is shown by aggregated figures for all the provinces as follows:—

Provincial Revenues and Expenditures, 1873-1925

Fiscal years ended	Ordinary revenue	Ordinary expenditure
	$	$
1873	6,960,922	6,868,884
1881	7,858,698	8,119,701
1891	10,693,815	11,628,353
1901	14,074,991	14,146,059
1911	40,706,948	38,144,511
1921	102,030,458	102,569,515
1925	132,398,729	136,648,242

Municipal Government and Finance.—Under the British North America Act, the municipalities are the creations of the Provincial Governments. Their basis of organization and their powers differ widely in different provinces, but almost everywhere they have very considerable powers of local self-government. If we include the local government districts of Saskatchewan and Alberta, there are over 4,100 municipal governments in Canada. These 4,100 municipal governments have together probably 20,000 members described as mayors, reeves, controllers, councillors, etc., and experience in municipal government trains men for the wider duties of public life in the Dominion and in the provinces. Certain of the larger municipalities, indeed, are larger spenders of public money than are the provinces themselves. For example, the annual gross expenditure of Toronto and Montreal is greater than that of Ontario and Quebec, the provinces in which they are respectively situated.

The cost of municipal government, like the cost of the provincial and Dominion government, has greatly increased in recent years, as a result of the diminished purchasing power of the dollar and larger expenditures on education and other public services. Thus the aggregate taxes imposed by the municipalities of Ontario increased from $34,231,214 in 1913 to $97,941,850 in 1925. In Quebec the aggregate ordinary expenditures of the municipalities increased from $19,139,465 in 1914 to $49,257,236 in 1925. In Manitoba, again, municipal taxation has increased from $9,922,537 in 1912 to $18,265,773 in 1925. Similar increases have occurred in most of the other provinces.

Provincial Armorial Bearings

PRINCE EDWARD ISLAND

NOVA SCOTIA

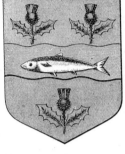

NEW BRUNSWICK

QUEBEC

ONTARIO

MANITOBA

SASKATCHEWAN

ALBERTA

BRITISH COLUMBIA

CHAPTER IV.

POPULATION—GENERAL ECONOMIC PROGRESS SINCE CONFEDERATION

Population growth affords an excellent measure of general economic progress, and the present chapter is written with that fact in mind, each of the more important fields of economic activity being given a chapter to itself in the remainder of the handbook.

It may not be generally known that the credit of taking what was perhaps the first census of modern times belongs to Canada, the year being 1665 and the census that of the little colony of New France. A population of 3,215 souls was shown. By the date of the Conquest, nearly a hundred years later (1763), this had increased to 70,000, what is now the Maritime Provinces having another 20,000. When it is recalled that in England and France the first census was taken in 1801, and in the United States only in 1790, the statistical initiative of the nascent St. Lawrence colony may call for more than passing appreciation.

After the Conquest came the influx of the Loyalists and the gradual settlement of the country, so that Canada began the nineteenth century with a population of probably 250,000 or 260,000. Forty-seven years later the first Act calling for the taking of a census at regular intervals was passed. The first census thereunder was taken in 1851, so that in addition to numerous records of earlier dates we now have regular decennial censuses by provinces for the past three-quarters of a century. In 1851 the total was 2,384,919 for the territory now included in the Dominion of Canada. There was a very rapid development in the 'fifties, and an only less substantial increase in the 'sixties, with the result that the first census after Confederation (1871) saw the Dominion launched with a population of 3,689,257. For the Confederation year itself the estimate is 3,327,000.

At Confederation the Dominion comprised, of course, only the original four provinces of Nova Scotia, New Brunswick, Quebec and Ontario, and it may be well to insert at this point reference tables which show the growth in population from decade to decade thereafter.

Growth of Population in Canada, 1867-1927

Provinces	1867	1871	1881	1891
Ontario	1,530,000[1]	1,620,851	1,926,922	2,114,321
Quebec	1,160,000[1]	1,191,516	1,359,027	1,488,535
New Brunswick	272,000[1]	285,594	321,233	321,263
Nova Scotia	365,000[1]	387,800	440,572	450,396
British Columbia	[3]	36,247	49,459	98,173
Prince Edward Island	81,000[1]	94,021	108,891	109,078
Manitoba	17,000[2]	25,228	62,260	152,506
Saskatchewan	[3]	[3]	[3]	[3]
Alberta	[3]	[3]	[3]	[3]
Yukon	[3]	[3]	[3]	[3]
North West Territories	[3]	48,000	56,446	98,967
Total		3,689,257	4,324,810	4,833,239

Provinces	1901	1911	1921	1927
Ontario	2,182,947	2,527,292	2,933,662	3,187,000
Quebec	1,648,898	2,005,776	2,361,199	2,604,000
New Brunswick	331,120	351,889	387,876	411,000
Nova Scotia	459,574	492,338	523,837	543,000
British Columbia	178,657	392,480	524,582	575,000
Prince Edward Island	103,259	93,728	88,615	87,000
Manitoba	255,211	461,394	610,118	647,000
Saskatchewan	91,279	492,432	757,510	836,000
Alberta	73,022	374,295	588,454	617,000
Yukon	27,219	8,512	4,157	3,470
North West Territories	20,129	6,507	7,988	9,050
Total	5,371,315	7,206,643	8,788,483[4]	9,519,520

[1] Estimated on basis of Census, 1861.
[2] Estimated on basis of Census, 1856.
[3] No figures of population for earlier years available upon which to base estimates of population for 1867.
[4] Includes 485 Canadian Navy.

Population of the Dominion in 1867, etc., and in 1927[1]

Provinces	Total		Per square mile	
	At organization or admission	In 1927	At organization or admission	In 1927
Original Confederation—				
Ontario	1,531,000	3,187,000	15.05	8.71
Quebec	1,160,000	2,604,000	6.19	3.77
New Brunswick	272,000	411,000	9.75	14.73
Nova Scotia	365,000	543,000	17.32	25.77
Admitted—				
British Columbia	36,000	575,000	0.10	1.63
Prince Edward Island	97,000	87,000	44.41	39.84
Organized—				
Manitoba	25,000	647,000	1.79	2.79
Saskatchewan	234,000	836,000	0.96	3.43
Alberta	169,000	617,000	0.67	2.44
Territories	48,000[2]	13,000	0.02	0.01

[1] See also table on page 12.
[2] Area and estimate of population are for 1871.

It is sometimes overlooked that the urge to Confederation was economic as well as political, as one of the main objects of union was to secure an offset to the loss of reciprocity. The first two years of the Dominion's life were, largely from this cause, years of dull times, but from 1869 to 1873 there was general prosperity reflecting the world-wide railway building boom, the construction of the Suez Canal and the industrial development of Germany. Canada during this period found many new markets, both foreign and interprovincial; nineteen new banks began business between Confederation and 1874. After 1873, due again largely to outside influence, Canada entered a period of depression, losing some of her foreign markets, though conditions were later somewhat alleviated by the completion of the Intercolonial, and still later by that of the Canadian Pacific Railway, which inaugurated the first and short-lived western boom. The adoption of a protective tariff in 1878 also stimulated manufactures, but on the whole business continued depressed throughout the later 'seventies, the whole of the 'eighties and the first part of the 'nineties. Notwithstanding many evidences of growth, some of them considerable, economic conditions in general were not marked by buoyancy until close upon the end of the century.

The censuses of 1881, 1891 and 1901 reflect these conditions. That of 1881 showed a gain of 635,553 or 17·23 per cent, but in neither of the two next following was this record equalled, the gains in each being under 550,000 or 12 per cent. With the end of the century the population of Canada had reached but 5⅓ millions, though at Confederation, when the economic resources of the country were being appraised and measured, expectation had set a figure very much higher as the goal for 1900.

It is within the present century, however, that the spectacular expansion of the Canadian population and general economic body has taken place. The outstanding initial feature was, of course, the opening of the "last best West." It is true that western population had doubled in each of the decades following the completion of the Canadian Pacific Railway. With 1900, however, this movement became greatly accelerated. There occurred at this juncture a great broadening in world credit. Capital in huge amounts began to flow from Great Britain to undeveloped countries throughout the world, and especially to Canada, who received a total of $2½ billions within a dozen years. (Total outside capital at present invested in Canada reaches $5¼ billions.) The immigration movement, which had seldom previously exceeded 30,000, and never 50,000 per annum, rose to over five times that volume, totalling in the ten years 1903-1913 over 2,500,000, which was perhaps as many as had previously entered the country in all the years back to Confederation. Two new trans-

Corner of King and Yonge Sts., Toronto, in 1815 and in 1927
Can. Govt. Motion Picture Bureau and J. Ross Robertson Collection

Corner of Main St. and Portage Ave., Winnipeg, in 1872 and in 1927
Public Archives and Can. Govt. Motion Picture Bureau

continental railways were begun. Simultaneously with this western development came an almost equally rapid expansion in the industrial centres of eastern Canada. Not all of the "boom" was wisely directed, and some reaction was felt in 1913. Then came the war. Its results were by no means purely destructive economically. The liquidation of excess development continued and the industrial and production structure of Canada was greatly strengthened by the new demands for food and war materials. Immigration, however, fell off to a point not much above a third of the immediately pre-war period. After a post-war boom in 1920, conditions slumped economically for three years, but we are now experiencing what there is reason to believe is a strong and permanent recovery.

The general population increase in Canada in the opening decade of the present century was 34 per cent, the fastest rate of any country in the world. In the second decade we grew 22 per cent, again the fastest rate with the one exception of Australia, whose growth was greater than ours by only a fraction of one per cent. A century earlier the United States grew 35 per cent decade by decade until 1860, but with this exception there has been no example of more rapid national progress than that of Canada according to her last two censuses. Since Confederation, Canada's population has nearly trebled, growing very nearly four times as fast as the world as a whole.

In 1881 the centre of population, east and west, was in the County of Prescott, Ontario, not far from the village of Caledonia. In 1891 it had moved west to the vicinity of Ottawa, where it remained until 1911, when it reached the County of Victoria. It is probably in Simcoe County at the present time. In 1871, only 2·96 per cent of the population dwelt west of the Lake of the Woods. In 1921 it was 28·37 per cent—2,500,000 people compared with 110,000 at Confederation.

There are numerous features, social as well as economic, that invite analysis in a record of progress like the above. The average Canadian family is about one member smaller than at Confederation. The average or median Canadian is about five years older, a change which reflects the smaller proportion of children, largely, due in turn to the lengthening of adult life and the immigration movement. There is a greater masculine superiority from the same cause. In racial composition British stocks are now 55 per cent of the whole instead of 60 (the decline has been chiefly in the Irish element) and the French 28 per cent instead of 31 per cent; other than British stocks, chiefly from continental Europe, have doubled, rising from 7 or 8 per cent to 15 per cent. As between rural and urban distribution the change is perhaps more striking than in any other field. Though we are predominantly agricultural, our town dwellers now all but equal the numbers upon the land (4,352,122 urban and 4,436,361 rural in

POPULATION OF CANADA 1871–1921.

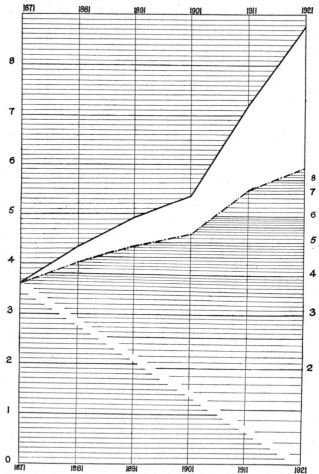

THE SOLID LINE IS ON AN ORDINARY SCALE REPRESENTING ACTUAL
GROWTH; THE DOTTED IS ON A LOGARITHMIC SCALE REPRESENTING RELATIVE
GROWTH, FROM DECADE TO DECADE. THE FIGURES OPPOSITE EACH LINE
REPRESENT MILLIONS ON THEIR RESPECTIVE SCALES.

1921); fifty years ago the towns and cities of Canada accounted for only 18 per cent of the people (686,019 urban and 3,003,238 rural), and at the beginning of the present century the percentage was but 37. In 1871 the Dominion had 13 cities, 49 towns, and 106 villages; in 1921 there were 101 cities, 462 towns, and 882 incorporated villages. It is the larger cities that have grown the fastest. There was no Calgary, Edmonton or Vancouver in 1867; Winnipeg was a collection of huts, and Toronto and Montreal were not one-sixth of their present size, though Halifax, Saint John and Quebec show less extraordinary contrasts. Another significant change is in occupations; increasing specialization, with the increased use of machinery, has been in progress for fifty years, with the result that the finance, trade and transportation occupations now bulk many times larger, proportionately, than they did at Confederation. The proportion of women employed in gainful occupations is probably twice as great as sixty years ago.

Origins of the People in 1871 and 1921

NOTE.—The figures for 1871 are for the four original provinces (Ontario, Quebec, New Brunswick, Nova Scotia) only.

Origins	1871	1921
	No.	No.
British—		
English	706,369	2,545,496
Irish	846,414	1,107,817
Scotch	549,946	1,173,637
Other	7,773	41,953
Total British	2,110,502	4,868,903
French	1,082,940	2,452,751
Dutch	29,662	117,506
German	202,991	294,636
Hebrew	125	126,196
Indian	23,035	110,814
Italian	1,035	66,769
Negro	21,496	18,291
Russian	607	100,064
Scandinavian[1]	1,623	167,359
Swiss	2,962	12,837
Various	1,222	431,108[2]
Unspecified	7,561	21,249
Grand Total	3,485,761	8,788,483

[1] Includes Danish, Icelandic, Norwegian and Swedish.

[2] Includes 107,671 Austrians, 39,587 Chinese, 15,868 Japanese, 53,403 Polish, 100,064 Russians, 106,721 Ukrainians, etc.

Birthplaces of the People in 1871 and 1921

Birthplaces	1871	1921
TOTAL POPULATION	3,485,761 [1]	8,788,483
British-born	3,391,093	7,898,201
Canadian-born	2,902,359	6,832,747
Prince Edward Island	7,768 [2]	101,513
Nova Scotia	360,832	506,824
New Brunswick	245,068	378,902
Quebec	1,147,664	2,266,062
Ontario	1,138,794	2,505,562
Manitoba		351,444
Saskatchewan		314,830
Alberta	405	211,643
British Columbia		167,169
Yukon		1,751
North West Territories		6,919
Not stated	1,828	20,128
British Isles	486,376	1,025,121
England and Wales	144,999	700,530
Ireland	219,451	93,301
Scotland	121,074	226,483
Lesser Isles	852	4,807
British Possessions	1,928	39,680
Foreign-born	94,668	890,282
Austria	102	57,535
France	2,899	19,249
Germany	24,162	25,266
Italy	218	35,531
Russia and Poland	416	130,334
Sweden, Norway, Denmark	588	58,019
United States	64,447	374,024
Asia	3	53,636
Other Countries	1,836	136,688
At Sea	430 [4]	653 [4]

[1] Nova Scotia, New Brunswick, Quebec and Ontario.
[2] Including Newfoundland.
[3] Included with other countries.
[4] Included with British-born.

Religions of the People, 1871 and 1921

Religions	1871 [1]	1921
Anglicans	494,049	1,407,994
Baptists	239,343	421,731
Confucians		27,114
Congregationalists	21,829	30,730
Greek Church	18	169,832
Jews	1,115	125,197
Lutherans	37,935	286,458
Mennonites		58,797
Methodists	567,091	1,159,458
Presbyterians	544,998	1,409,407
Protestants	10,146	30,754
Roman Catholics	1,492,029	3,389,636
Various Sects	77,208 [3]	271,375 [2]

[1] Four original provinces only.
[2] Having less than 25,000 adherents each.
[3] Having less than 16,000 adherents each.

For the economist, prices afford one of the best indexes of current phenomena; their general progress since Confederation gives special confirmation to the preceding brief sketch. The Dominion came into being at a time of falling prices. After 1870, however, influenced by the factors above described, Canada shared in the general prosperity, and prices rose. From 1874 to 1896 there was an unprecedented fall, Canada participating in this movement to the extent of a drop of at

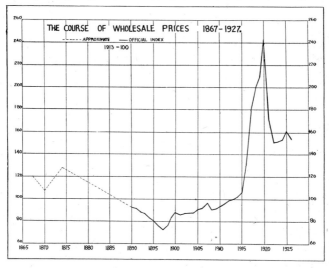

least 50 points, attributable to monetary factors (scarcity of gold, demonetization of silver, contraction of credit), the great increase in production generally, and improved transportation facilities. Based on 1913, the index of general prices was 120·0 in 1867 and 126·0 in 1874; by 1896 it had fallen to 76·0. From this point until 1913 prices again tended upward. It was a period of rapid and unprecedented prosperity almost the world over, and with the rising tide of trade prices rose steeply. The outstanding monetary factor was the heavy output of gold from the Transvaal, and an enlargement and development of credit systems based upon gold. On the basis of 1913, the general price level in 1896 was 76·0; by 1912 it had risen to 99·5, a gain of over 23 points. In 1913 a slump developed until the great war, during which the rise of prices was again stupendous. With the end of the war came a momentary lull, but in 1919 and the early part of 1920 the post-war boom carried the level higher than ever. In May, 1920, the index number was 256·7. The reaction from the optimism which had hoped too much from an impoverished world, drove prices precipitately downward until in December, 1921, the index was 150·6. For the three years, 1922-24, it remained comparatively stable, but jumped to 160·3 in 1925. During 1926 the course has been downward, partly due to the return of several countries to the gold standard, and to lower prices for certain foods and raw materials. A favourable feature in recent years has been the removal of the disparity between prices of commodities produced by the farmer and those which he has to buy.

The above is a record mainly of material progress, but man does not live by bread alone. Even more profound has been the change in the social and political order. The standard of everyday living has altered in numerous directions, and on the whole has greatly risen. We have much more leisure. There have been great advances in education. The spiritual side of life has been developed. A literature distinctly Canadian has sprung up. A vigorous school of Canadian painting exists. Canada has played her part in the progress of science and inventions which is one of the features of the century. The death rate has greatly declined. Perhaps most representative of all is the evolution of a Canadian national consciousness as a great self-governing community within the British Commonwealth, at the same time that a series of new relationships have been worked out with the other countries of the world, more particularly with the adjacent republic of the United States, with whom international amity and neighbourly good fellowship have been cultivated in a spirit and to a degree that is unique. The seal upon Canadian nationhood was set by the war. For it Canada raised 595,000 men (418,000 of whom went overseas); she supplied the Allies with over $1,002,000,000 worth of munitions, besides doubling her food exports; in the Patriotic Fund, Red Cross and other voluntary subscriptions she raised about $100,000,000; while publicly she incurred financial responsibility amounting in the aggregate to nearly two billions of dollars. From this great effort she has emerged without permanent disability and indeed with every prospect of a development that will eclipse the past.

CHAPTER V.—GENERAL SURVEY OF CANADIAN WEALTH, PRODUCTION AND INCOME

A general survey of our national wealth, production and income may well precede a more detailed review of the more important fields of economic progress in Canada. According to the latest estimate (1921), the tangible wealth of the Dominion apart from undeveloped natural resources amounts at present to about $22 billions. There is no earlier figure that is strictly comparable, but it is fairly certain that at Confederation our national wealth was under $1½ billions. Agricultural values make up about $8 billions of the present total, urban real estate nearly $6 billions, and the railways considerably over $2 billions. Ontario owns about one-third, Quebec about one-quarter, and Saskatchewan about one-eighth. (*See* tables herewith for complete statement by items and by provinces.)

An Estimate of the National Wealth of Canada

Classification of wealth	Aggregate amount	Percentage of total	Average amount per head of population
Farm values (land, buildings, implements, machinery and live stock, census, 1921)....	$ 6,586,648,126	p.c. 29.68	$ 749
Agricultural products in the possession of farmers and traders, 1921......................	1,396,223,000	6.29	159
Total Agricultural Wealth, 1921........	7,982,871,126	35.97	908
Mines (capital employed, 1921)...............	559,514,154	2.52	64
Forests (estimated value of accessible raw materials, pulpwood and capital invested in woods operations)......................	1,197,660,000	5.40	136
Fisheries (capital invested in boats, gear, etc., in primary operations, 1921)................	25,648,650	0.12	3
Central electric stations (capital invested, 1921)	239,675,661	1.08	27
Manufactures (machinery and tools, 1921).....	610,068,624	2.75	70
Manufactures (materials on hand, stocks in process; estimate for amount in dealers' hands, 1921)...................................	1,362,535,764	6.14	155
Steam railways (investment in road and equipment).....................................	2,159,298,000	9.73	246
Electric railways (investment in road and equipment)................................	186,519,439	0.84	21
Canals (amount expended on construction to March 31, 1922)...........................	141,425,373	0.64	16
Telephones (cost of property and equipment)..	158,678,229	0.71	18
Urban real property (assessed valuations and exempted property and estimated for under valuation by assessors, and for roads, sewers, etc.)...................................	5,751,505,257	25.91	654
Shipping (estimated from 1918 census and distributed according to tonnage owned).......	100,000,000	0.45	11
Imported merchandise in store, being one half imports during year 1921....................	373,902,166	1.68	43
Household furnishings, clothing, carriages, motors, etc., distributed according to wealth and population............................	1,144,000,000	5.15	130
Specie held by Government and Chartered Banks and estimated for public holdings....	202,000,000	0.91	23
Total Estimated Wealth, 1921.........	22,195,302,443	100.00	2,525

Provincial Distribution of the National Wealth of Canada, with Percentage and Per Capita Analyses

Provinces	Estimated wealth	Percentage distribution of wealth	Wealth per capita
	$	p.c.	$
Prince Edward Island	119,912,060	0.5	1,353
Nova Scotia	752,697,986	3.4	1,437
New Brunswick	597,596,369	2.7	1,541
Quebec	5,541,819,967	25.0	2,347
Ontario	7,353,397,816	33.1	2,507
Manitoba	1,650,495,868	7.4	2,705
Saskatchewan	2,845,642,985	12.8	3,757
Alberta	1,950,973,479	8.8	3,317
British Columbia	1,365,896,120	6.2	2,604
Yukon	16,869,792	0.1	4,058
Canada	22,195,302,443	100.0	2,525

Production and Income.—Under the term "production" are usually included the activities of agriculture, fishing, mining, forestry, power development, manufactures and construction. This does not imply that many other activities, such as transportation, merchandizing, professional services, etc., are not also "productive" in a broad economic sense; at bottom it is the sum total of all economic activities that creates the national income. It is usual, however, to regard the processes that consist in the creation of materials or their making over into new forms as constituting "production" in a special sense, and it is of this that a bird's eye view is given in the table on page 46 which shows the gross and net value of production in each of the divisions of industry above mentioned. In a second table a summary of the value of total production in Canada by provinces is given.

It will be seen that agriculture and manufactures rank as rivals for first place in net value of production for the whole of Canada, with forestry and mining in third and fourth place respectively, though construction operations in certain years rise higher than mining. By provinces, Ontario and Quebec occupy first place, largely because of their manufacturing pre-eminence, with the three Prairie Provinces following—the result of their large agricultural output.

As these industries engage only two-thirds of those gainfully employed in Canada it would be safe to add one-half to the figures to obtain the value of all productive activities—a concept which approximates to that of the national income, which we may thus put down at upwards of $4 billions. Figures for comprehensive comparison at Confederation are lacking, but it would be safe to say that our general productive capacity has increased by ten times.

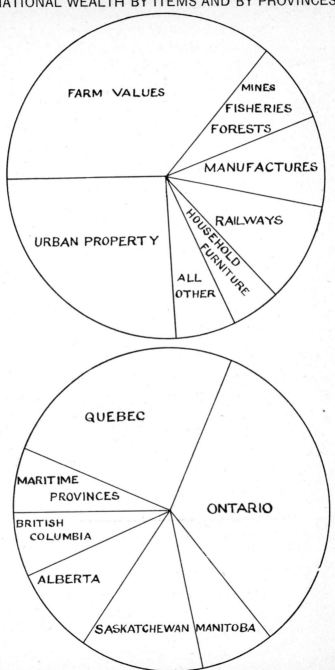

Summary by Industries of the Value of Production in Canada, 1924

Industry	Gross	Net [1]	Per cent of total net
	$	$	p.c.
Agriculture	1,530,481,735	1,140,895,500	37.8
Forestry	433,816,948	311,265,847	10.3
Fisheries	56,014,651	44,534,235	1.5
Trapping	14,785,634	14,785,634	0.5
Mining	230,016,492	209,583,406	6.9
Electric Power	95,169,768	74,616,863	2.5
Total Primary Production	2,360,285,228	1,795,681,485	59.5
Construction	287,687,809	187,114,415	6.2
Custom and Repair	90,837,351	58,053,266	1.9
Manufactures[2]	2,695,053,582	1,256,643,901	32.4
Total Secondary Production[2]	3,073,578,742	1,501,811,582	40.5
Grand Total[2]	4,930,417,387	3,018,182,081	100.0

[1] Gross value minus value of materials consumed in the production process.
[2] The item "Manufactures" includes dairy factories, sawmills, pulpmills, fish canning and curing, shipbuilding and certain mineral industries, which are also included in other headings above. This duplication, amounting to a gross of $503,446,583 and a net of $279,310,986, is eliminated from the grand total.

Summary by Provinces of the Value of Production in Canada, 1924

Province	Gross	Net [1]	Per cent of total net
	$	$	p.c.
Prince Edward Island	24,378,343	18,138,381	0.6
Nova Scotia	145,356,067	96,071,433	3.2
New Brunswick	127,429,891	78,298,070	2.5
Quebec	1,207,316,656	729,992,866	24.1
Ontario	2,147,755,210	1,217,764,312	40.0
Manitoba	279,328,851	190,022,463	6.8
Saskatchewan	330,903,240	237,254,471	7.7
Alberta	298,589,566	210,972,370	6.7
British Columbia	366,499,403	236,816,575	7.5
Yukon	2,860,160	2,851,140	0.9
Canada	4,930,417,387	3,018,182,081	100.0

[1] Gross value minus value of materials consumed in the production process.

CHAPTER VI.—AGRICULTURE

The first cultivation of the soil in Canada was at Annapolis, N.S., under de Monts in 1605, when some vegetables were grown. But the first real Canadian farmer was Louis Hébert, who landed in 1617 and began to clear land at a spot now in the middle of Upper Town, Quebec. His tools were an axe and a spade, but he planted both seed and apple trees. Three joined him in the following year. In another twenty years there were several hundreds. In half a century the "habitants" (as they were called from a very early date) had 11,000 acres under crop and 3,000 cattle. So in the other provinces, each had its small beginnings and early struggles. Passing entirely over history (including such major incidents as the settlement of the Loyalists and the first opening of the West) we may come at once to Confederation and the comparison with present-day Canadian agriculture.

1. Field Crops

At the first Census (1871), the agriculture of Canada (Nova Scotia, New Brunswick, Quebec and Ontario) recorded only the areas under wheat, hay and potatoes, these being respectively 1,646,781 acres, 3,650,419 acres, and 403,102 acres. Thus we cannot comprehensively compare crop acreages with those of to-day. In yields, wheat then occupied a secondary position, oats yielding 42,489,453 bushels, wheat 16,723,873 bushels, barley 11,496,068 bushels and peas 9,905,720 bushels. None of the other grains reached 5 million bushels. The yield of potatoes was 28,398,112 cwt., of field roots 16,735,642 cwt., and of hay 3,818,641 tons.

It is in respect of the principal grain crops, and especially of wheat, that agricultural progress during the past sixty years has been most remarkable. For ten years after Confederation, the Canadian wheat crop rarely, if ever, exceeded 25 million bushels, and imports of wheat and flour exceeded exports by nearly 9 million bushels. The home production of wheat did not in fact quite suffice for domestic requirements. Afterwards a gradual increase in production became apparent, and exports began decidedly to exceed imports; yet it was not until 1898 that the wheat yield exceeded 50 million bushels, and exports reached what was then the record total of 24½ million bushels.

In 1886 occurred the epoch-making event of the completion of the Canadian Pacific Railway, which, linking east and west and causing the great Dominion to become for the first time a real economic unit, also opened up the great prairie lands of the middle West, with their

47

soils of virginal fertility. Up to 1880 the bulk of the wheat of Canada was grown in Ontario, but the Prairie Provinces have since gradually come to produce nearly all the wheat of the Dominion. Thus in 1870, 85 per cent of the wheat of Canada was grown in Ontario; this proportion is now little more than 5 per cent, whilst in Saskatchewan the proportion increased from 4 per cent in 1890 to 53 per cent in 1926. A similar change is observable in the case of barley and oats. Up to 1880 production was almost entirely confined to Eastern Canada; in 1926, for barley 82 per cent, and for oats 57½ per cent of the total crop was grown in the Prairie Provinces. The first carload of western wheat left Winnipeg for Montreal by the new all-Canadian railway only in December, 1885.

Acreages.—In 1890 the area under field crops for all Canada was 15,662,811 acres. The census showed an increase to 19,763,740 acres in 1900, to 30,556,168 acres in 1910, and to 47,553,418 acres in 1920. For the year 1926, the total area under field crops in Canada was estimated to be 56,927,371 acres; so that from 1890 to 1926 the area under field crops has grown from about 15·6 million acres to close upon 57 million acres, an increase of 41·4 million acres, or 263 per cent during the last 36 years. This was largely due to the opening of the West, but the war also caused a wonderful manifestation of farming energy, for within the period 1913 to 1919 alone the area under field crops grew from 35·4 to 53 million acres, or by about 50 per cent, notwithstanding the decline of immigration and the absence of a large proportion of Canadian manhood overseas.

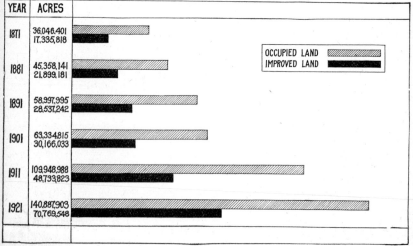

AREA OF OCCUPIED AND IMPROVED LANDS 1871–1921

YEAR	ACRES
1871	36,046,401 / 17,335,818
1881	45,358,141 / 21,899,181
1891	58,997,995 / 28,537,242
1901	63,334,815 / 30,166,033
1911	109,948,988 / 48,733,823
1921	140,887,903 / 70,769,548

OCCUPIED LAND
IMPROVED LAND

Wheat.—Reverting to wheat, we have noted its growth from a crop of, say, 20 million bushels at Confederation to one of 55½ millions at the end of the century. The first year in which production exceeded 100 million bushels was 1905. From 1911 to 1913 there were three good years in succession, with yields well over 200 million bushels. A poor harvest in 1914 was followed in 1915 by the phenomenal record of 393½ million bushels, the average yield per acre being 26 bushels— a rate never before or since reached (though the average yield in Alberta in 1923 was 28 bushels). During five of the last six years (1921 to 1926) the total of 1915 has been four times exceeded, viz., in 1922 (nearly 400 million bushels); in 1923 (474 million bushels); in 1925 (411 million bushels); and in 1926 (410 million bushels). Thus, taking the extreme limits of the sixty-year period, the production of wheat has grown from the insignificant total of 21·3 million bushels in 1868 to 474 million bushels in the peak year 1923 and to well over 400 million bushels during each of the last two years.

Other Grains.—Whilst wheat stands supreme as a staple of human food, the other grain crops are of scarcely less importance for the maintenance of the live stock industry. Their volume of production, especially in the case of oats, has attained very considerable dimensions. Oats, of which in 1870 not more than about 42½ million bushels were grown, reached the record total of close upon 564 million bushels in 1923; the area under crop has expanded from 3,961,356 acres in

Miles of Stooked Wheat in Western Canada

Photo by Can. Govt. Motion Picture Bureau

1890 to 14,672,320 acres in 1925. Barley, the production of which was 11,496,000 bushels in 1870, yielded the record total of 112,668,000 bushels in 1925.

Improvement in Methods.—Progress in the cultivation of field crops has not been confined to expansion of area and increase of volume. The production of better varieties of grain and improvement in the methods of cultivation have also been of great importance under the scientific and educational activities of the Dominion and Provincial Departments of Agriculture. In this connection the work of the Dominion Experimental Farms may be specially mentioned. Begun only in 1886, at the present time the Experimental Farms and Stations number 24, with a total acreage of 12,783, as compared with a total acreage on the five original farms of 3,472. It would be impossible even to enumerate, much less describe, these operations here; but in connection with Canada's great wheat-growing industry one outstanding achievement deserves special mention. Wheat of the Prairie Provinces is famous for its hard, dry, glutinous quality. Apart from the effects of climate and soil, its success has been largely due to the excellence of the Red Fife variety, which was discovered accidentally in 1842 by an Ontario farmer named David Fife. In 1903, however, an improved variety known as "Marquis" was produced by the Cereal Division of the Central Experimental Farm at Ottawa. During the last ten years the success of this variety has been such that it has now almost entirely superseded the Red Fife. The Marquis is remarkable for length of straw, comparative freedom from rust, heavy weight per bushel, fine appearance of grain, and excellent colour and baking strength of flour, whilst above all the fact that it ripens about a week earlier than the Red Fife renders it immensely valuable through increased safety from frost. The use of this new variety of wheat has increased by millions of dollars annually the revenue derived from wheat-growing by the farmers of Western Canada. A still more recent product is a variety called "Garnet". This is now being tried and multiplied upon an extensive scale. It matures earlier even than the Marquis, and great hopes are entertained of its future.

The Canadian Grain Trade.—Keeping pace with production have been the efforts to market efficiently and expeditiously the ever-increasing volume of the prairie-grown wheat. When it is remembered that the market for this product is distant about 5,000 miles of land and ocean from the points of production, the achievement of the Dominion in exporting to Europe at a profit is remarkable. It is indeed in the production of wheat for export that Canada has made the greatest progress during the period under review. The development of the Canadian grain trade, especially since the opening of the present century, has been phenomenally rapid. In no country of the world are the arrangements for the inspection and grading of grain more thorough and complete, the certificates of the government inspectors being accepted everywhere as *prima facie* evidence of the quality of the grain. From 1874 until 1925, legislation has been continuously improved. In 1912 provision was first made for the appointment of the Board of Grain Commissioners, charged with the management and control of the grain trade for the whole of Canada. The Act governs the operation of the licensed grain elevators, the growth in number and capacity of which alone affords striking evidence of the development of the trade. Thus at the end of the last century the total number of grain elevators and warehouses in Canada was 523 with a capacity of 18,329,352 bushels; for 1925 the number was 4,416 and the capacity 281,746,560 bushels. The total exports of wheat and wheat flour have grown from 5,276,898 bushels in 1870 to 309,587,418 bushels in 1924 and 295,061,853 bushels in 1926, counting by fiscal years. With the elimination of Russia as an important wheat-exporting country, Canada has become the world's second largest wheat-producing and also wheat-exporting country, the United States being first. As a wheat-producing country Canada has occupied the second place in four out of the last five crop years ended July 31, and as a wheat-exporting country the Dominion has been first three times and second three times during the six crop years ended July 31, 1926, its total exports in these six

Government Terminal Elevator, Head of Lakes
Photo by Can. Govt. Motion Picture Bureau

years, including wheat flour expressed as wheat, reaching 1,496 million bushels, as compared with 1,372 million bushels exported from the United States. The Canadian record for volume of wheat exports was made in the crop year of 1923-24, when 346,521,561 bushels were exported after the bumper harvest of 1923. For the crop year 1925-26, the almost equally large export was made of 324,592,021 bushels. See diagram opposite for channels through which the Canadian wheat crop reaches market.

Western Wheat Pools.—Important developments have occurred in western Canada during the last four years by the organization of what are popularly known as "Wheat Pools", which represent a form of co-operative marketing by producers. The grain producers of the Prairie Provinces had previously co-operated in the ownership and working of grain elevators, the Saskatchewan Co-operative Elevator Company, established in 1911, and the United Grain Growers, established in 1918, handling between them in a large grain year something like 73 million bushels. The formation of the wheat pools is a further development of the same principle. The inspiration of the enterprise was apparently supplied by the success of the Government control of grain marketing during the war, which control ceased in 1920. The three voluntary western wheat pools began operations, Alberta on October 29, 1923, Saskatchewan on September 8, 1924, and Manitoba on January 28, 1924. In 1924 representatives of each organized a central selling agency under a Dominion charter with the title of the Canadian Co-operative Wheat Producers, Ltd. The method of working is to secure five-year contracts with as many wheat growers as possible for disposal of all the wheat grown by them, with the exception of the quantities reserved for seed and food. A fixed sum per bushel on the basis of the price for No. 1 Northern is paid by interim instalments and by final payments according to the price realized and after the deduction of expenses of marketing and of an elevator and commercial reserve. The claim made for the pools is that better prices are obtained for the members than by the ordinary system of marketing. At the third annual meeting of the Manitoba Pool held in 1926 it was reported that the total wheat handled by the central selling agency of the three western Pools was approximately 190 million bushels. The pool system has lately been extended to coarse grains, of which 26 million bushels are reported as having been handled by the central selling agency during the first year of operation.

Special Crops.—In addition to the ordinary crops grown on a field scale, there are a number of special crops suited to particular localities which in the aggregate represent an important contribution to Canada's agricultural wealth. Their cultivation has either been initiated or greatly increased since Confederation. They comprise

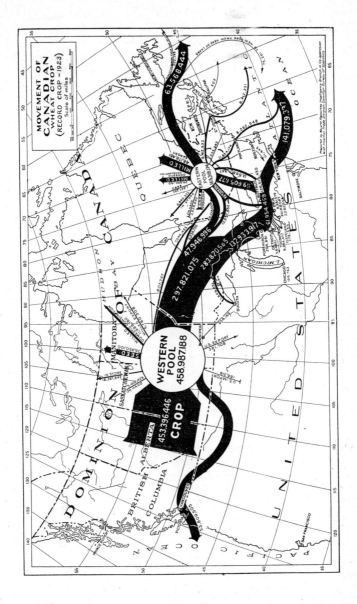

tobacco in Quebec and Ontario; maple syrup and sugar in Eastern Canada; sugar beets for beet sugar, and flax for fibre in Ontario. Tobacco, now grown principally in Quebec and Ontario, is annually increasing in importance. A production of 11,267,000 lb. from 11,906 acres in 1900 has increased to 28,824,000 lb. from 33,356 acres in 1926. Maple syrup and maple sugar are produced annually to the value of about $5,000,000, of which about 63 per cent is produced in Quebec. Sugar beets are now grown in Ontario, where there are two sugar beet factories, and in Alberta, where there is now one such factory. The earliest attempts to establish a beet sugar industry in Canada were made about 36 years ago and for some time large beet sugar factories were operated at Farnham, Coaticook, and elsewhere in Quebec, under bounties from the Dominion Government. Again, in 1902 four beet sugar companies began operations in Ontario, and from 1903 to 1914 a sugar beet factory also operated in Alberta. In 1911, 175,000 tons were grown upon 20,677 acres. Since that date the production of beets has ranged from 71,000 tons in 1916 to 370,000 tons in 1925. The production of refined beetroot sugar, which was 21,329,680 lb. in 1911, reached a maximum of 89,280,719 lb. in 1920, and was 72,819,919 lb. in 1925. The value of the sugar reached a maximum between 1918 and 1925, being $12,856,424 in 1920 (at 14·4 cents per lb.). The production of flax for fibre and fibre seed reached considerable dimensions during the war; in 1920 the production of fibre reached its maximum of 7,440,000 lb., with a value for fibre seed and by-products of $7,130,000. Of clover and grass seed the value in 1924 was $3,594,000. Hops are grown to the extent of 507 acres in British Columbia, the total yield during the last seven years ranging, according to the season, from 680,907 lb. in 1922 to 999,804 lb. in 1923.

Values of Field Crops, 1867-1927.—Prices of agricultural products reached their peak during and just after the war in 1919. They slumped steeply thereafter, falling to a very low level in 1923, recovering, however, considerably in recent years. With due allowance for these facts, it may yet be pointed out how great the contrast is between the value of field crops at Confederation, and that to which they have now attained. The value of the field crops of Canada in 1870 was estimated at the time to be $111,116,606. This figure had more than doubled in 1900, and in 1910 it had increased to $384,513,795. The amount reached $638,580,000 in 1914. As the effects of the war came to be felt, the maximum was reached in 1919 with a total of $1,537,-170,100. This value receded to $899,226,200 in 1923; but the recovery of prices during recent years, combined with excellent harvests, has brought the value up to $1,153,394,900 in 1925 and $1,121,447,100 in 1926.

Flour Mills in Canada.—Tke most important manufacturing industry connected with the field crops is flour-milling, which dates back
to the settlement made by the French at Port Royal (now Annapolis,
N.S.) in 1605, where in that year was erected the first water wheel to
turn a millstone on the North American continent north of Mexico.
Milling was, of course, an absolute necessity to the settlers; in Lower
Canada the seigneurs were compelled to build mills. The Napoleonic
wars established the export business, and for the next half-century
the mills were closely associated with the commercial and banking
history of the country. At Confederation there were 2,295 flour and
grist mills in Canada with a total capital of $9,929,898. Materials
used had a value of $32,474,548 and the value of products amounted
to $39,135,919.

Large scale production in milling in Canada began with competition
between the two processes, stone and roller milling. By the 'eighties
the roller process had secured a virtual monopoly, and local mills gave
way to large mills served by elevators at central points. The high
quality of Canadian wheat became recognized throughout the world,
and Canada's huge export trade in wheat and its products developed.
The milling industry grew apace. The latest figures available are for
1925 and show that since 1871, with the growth of large scale production, the number of mills has decreased to 1,310, including over
1,000 country mills which are still carrying on. But the capital invested
has grown to $60,104,258; the cost of raw materials to $163,164,668,
while the value of products is $187,944,731. The exports of wheat
flour in the fiscal year 1868-9 were 375,219 barrels valued at $1,948,696,
while in the fiscal year ended March 31, 1926, 10,084,974 barrels of
flour, valued at $69,687,598, were exported from Canada to other
countries. The quantity of flour exported has therefore increased over
25 times in the period of less than sixty years, while the value has
increased over 35 times.

The total daily capacity of flour mills in 1927 is nearly 125,000
barrels. Canada has to-day the largest flour mill in the British Empire,
with a daily capacity of 14,000 barrels. Our largest Canadian milling
company controls a daily capacity of 24,500 barrels.

2.—The Live Stock and Dairying Industries.

Although somewhat overshadowed by the grain-growing industry,
the raising of live stock has made very substantial progress not only
in point of numbers but by the improvement of breeding stock.
Fortunately, virulent animal diseases, which affect so disastrously
the farm live stock of Europe, have never obtained a footing in Canada.
It has been a matter of great satisfaction therefore that after many

years of agitation the removal of the embargo against the introduction of store cattle into Great Britain was secured in 1923. As a result, shipments of store cattle to this market for the fiscal year 1926 reached the total of 92,027, as compared with 53,061 in 1924-25, 28,151 in 1923-24 and 1,068 in 1922-23.

Numerically, since the first census after Confederation (1871), horses have increased from 836,743 to 3,558,849 in the year 1926; cattle from 2,621,290 to 9,160,150; and swine from 1,366,083 to 4,470,771. The number of sheep has fluctuated considerably; in 1871 it was 3,155,509, but for many years afterwards it declined. The highest number reached during the sixty years was 3,720,783 in 1920. At the present time (1926) sheep number only 3,035,507.

The Dairying Industry.—The establishment of the dairying industry upon a co-operative factory basis has been one of the most significant agricultural developments since Confederation. Co-operative dairy farming may indeed be regarded as the sheet anchor of present-day farming in Eastern Canada.

The dairy factory system in Canada had its origin in the 1850's· Of the cheese factories operating in 1900, the oldest was in Oxford South, Ont., dating back to 1855. The oldest factory in Quebec started at Missisquoi in 1866. The first Canadian creamery was started in Missisquoi in 1869, the second at Chateauguay in 1874, and the third in Waterloo North in the same year.

Dairy Farming in Eastern Canada

Photo by Can. Govt. Motion Picture Bureau

After Confederation the multiplication of cheese factories was fairly rapid, especially in Ontario, and production increased steadily until 1904, when a large increase in the consumption of milk and the diversion of milk to condenseries and milk powder factories resulted in some decrease in cheese production. The low point was reached in 1922.

The creamery system for the manufacture of butter has been of slower growth. Little progress was made until after 1882, when the first centrifugal cream separator used on the American continent was imported from Denmark and installed in a creamery at Ste. Marie, Beauce Co., Quebec. Another important development was the introduction about 1896 of mechanical refrigeration in cold storage warehouses, railway services and transatlantic steamers. The dairying industry in Eastern Canada has also owed much to the increasing use of fodder corn as a silage crop, which enabled the production of milk to be forced during the winter. Whilst dairying has been practised chiefly in Eastern Canada, very gratifying progress has been recently made in the Prairie Provinces, from which both cheese and butter are now being exported.

In 1870 the total value of the dairy products of Canada was estimated at $15,023,966. For the latest year available, the total value of these products is placed at $241,069,320, comprising butter $95,136,896, cheese $36,666,629, miscellaneous products $16,882,747, and milk consumed fresh $92,383,648. The number of milch cows in Canada has increased from 1,251,209 in 1870 to 3,951,335 in 1926.

Slaughtering and Meat Packing.—According to the census of 1871 there were 193 establishments engaged in slaughtering and meat packing with a capital of $419,325, employing 841 people who received $145,376 in salaries and wages. The cost of raw materials used was $2,942,786 and the value of the product $3,799,552. After 1900 the separation between the farm and the manufacture and marketing of animal products became more and more pronounced, leading to the development of a large scale industry, 1925 returns showing only 74 establishments engaged in slaughtering and meat packing, but with a capital of $54,316,043. The number of employees had increased to 10,709 and salaries and wages received by employees to $13,549,545. The cost of materials used in 1925 was $132,329,355 and the value of the product $163,816,310.

Exports of Live Stock and their Products.—Total exports of cattle in 1867 numbered 47,809, valued at $1,190,799, all to the United States; in 1926 total exports were 295,249 head valued at $18,081,479, of which $12,432,954 worth went to the United Kingdom and $5,338,737 worth went to the United States. Exports of swine numbered 8,790 valued at $41,350 in 1867, all to the United States; in 1926 the number had increased to 52,025 valued at $1,266,676, of which shipments to the value of $1,192,475 went to the United States. In 1867 shipments of bacon and hams amounted to 25,370 cwt. valued at $287,467, while in 1926 the quantity had increased to 1,253,760 cwt. valued at $28,590,301; exports to the United Kingdom were valued at $250,678 and $27,944,472 respectively.

The Alberta Ranch of H.R.H. The Prince of Wales

Photo by Can. Govt. Motion Picture Bureau

Dairy products are also exported from Canada in large quantities. In 1867, 14,081 cwt. of cheese valued at $193,554 were exported from Canada, while 1,483,335 cwt. valued at $33,718,587 were exported in 1926. Exports of butter in 1867 amounted to 10,817,918 lb. valued at $1,741,291, and in 1926 amounted to 23,303,865 lb. valued at $8,773,125, the larger part going to the United Kingdom.

Total exports of animals and animal products have increased in value from $6,118,639 in 1867 to $154,182,754 in 1926.

The sheep and wool industry, however, has remained practically stationary during this period. According to the census of 1870-1, 1,557,430 sheep were killed or sold off farms and 11,103,480 lb. of wool were sold. Corresponding figures from the census of 1920-1 show 1,217,987 and 11,338,268 lb. respectively. During the same period the number of cattle killed or sold off farms increased from 507,725 to 2,097,390, and the number of swine slaughtered from 1,216,097 to 2,972,331.

Fruit Trees in Blossom

3.—The Fruit-Growing Industry.

The Canadian climate and soil are eminently adapted for fruit-growing, and the Annapolis Valley, the Niagara Peninsula, and the Okanagan district, B.C., are world-famous. Experimental shipments of apples from the Annapolis Valley were first made in 1861. Up to 1890 the annual production of apples by Nova Scotia rarely exceeded 100,000 barrels; but after that date there was a pronounced increase in acreage and in production, which reached 1,000,000 barrels in 1909, and 1,900,000 barrels in 1911. Further high records were made in 1919 with over 2,000,000 barrels, and in 1922, when 1,891,850 barrels were packed and sold from the Annapolis Valley and adjacent districts. In Ontario, where the commercial production of all descriptions of fruit has reached its highest development, apples have been grown from the middle of the eighteenth century, but commercial orcharding has developed only during the past 50 or 60 years, and was only possible when the building of the railways permitted trees and fruit to be rapidly transported. In British Columbia commercial fruit-growing is of comparatively recent origin, but progress has been very rapid during the last ten years. The first apple trees were planted about 1850; but not until after completion of the Canadian Pacific Railway

Harvesting the Fruit Crop

in 1886 were there many trees planted for commercial purposes. In 1891 the area under all kinds of fruit in British Columbia was 6,500 acres; by 1921 this area had expanded to 43,569 acres.

In 1925 the total value of Canadian commercial fruits was $21,588,620, comprising apples $16,024,165; pears $332,735; plums and prunes $154,288; peaches $547,772; cherries $409,210; strawberries $1,460,650; raspberries $405,840; other berries $554,000 and grapes $1,680,000. For 1926, the value of commercial fruits is estimated preliminarily at $20,316,956, of which $13,728,120 is for apples.

Fruit and Vegetable Canning.—In 1925 there were 242 fruit and vegetable canneries representing a capital investment of $24,424,064, and with products valued at $22,376,313. This great industry is entirely a growth since Confederation.

4.—Grand Total of Agricultural Wealth and Production.

The estimated gross agricultural wealth of Canada is $7,508,257,-000. Annual estimates of the total gross value of agricultural production, made for the last ten years, show a total of over $1,600 millions to-day as compared with $1,100 millions in 1915. The tables herewith may be consulted for details, while for future possibilities the reader may be referred back to Chapter II.

A Relic of Confederation Days

Photo by Can. Govt. Motion Picture Bureau

Estimated Gross Agricultural Wealth of Canada, 1926

("000" omitted)

Province	Lands	Buildings	Implements and machinery	Live stock
	$	$	$	$
Prince Edward Island	28,476	17,289	6,870	8,877
Nova Scotia	49,155	51,173	10,146	19,355
New Brunswick	61,112	45,158	13,545	16,845
Quebec	546,666	285,530	111,940	131,618
Ontario	808,124	491,330	169,954	236,061
Manitoba	315,245	113,005	67,848	57,799
Saskatchewan	877,042	216,398	176,676	135,622
Alberta	523,221	121,765	98,814	98,021
British Columbia	107,020	41,036	9,379	20,457
Canada	3,316,061	1,382,684	665,172	724,655

Province	Poultry	Animals on fur farms	Agricultural production	Total
	$	$	$	$
Prince Edward Island	848	3,324	25,525	91,209
Nova Scotia	798	565	41,251	172,443
New Brunswick	973	979	36,786	175,393
Quebec	8,461	1,225	271,001	1,356,441
Ontario	20,177	1,808	482,481	2,209,935
Manitoba	3,955	652	147,050	705,554
Saskatchewan	7,121	178	364,840	1,777,877
Alberta	5,655	723	254,739	1,102,938
British Columbia	2,983	546	44,502	225,923
Canada	50,971	10,000	1,668,175	7,817,718

Estimated Gross Annual Agricultural Revenue of Canada, 1926

("000" omitted)

Items	1926
	$
Field crops	1,121,447
Farm animals	153,942
Wool	3,979
Dairy products	238,142
Fruits and vegetables	47,718
Poultry and eggs	78,867
Fur farming	4,363
Maple products	4,896
Tobacco	7,380
Flax fibre	450
Clover and grass seed	5,037
Honey	1,954
Totals	1,668,175

CHAPTER VII.—THE FOREST WEALTH OF CANADA

Of the total land area of Canada (approximately 3,650,000 square miles) about 1,227,000 square miles are covered by forests. Only about 40 per cent of this, however, carries merchantable timber (6″ in diameter), and only about 20 per cent carries saw timber (10″ in diameter), the rest being occupied by young stands which have come up after fire or cutting. The above area is estimated to contain 482,075 million feet board measure of saw material, and 1,279,705,000 cords of pulpwood, cordwood, poles, etc., making a total equivalent to 246,826 million cubic feet. Notwithstanding that we are still using or allowing timber to be destroyed by fire or by insects at the rate of 5 billion cubic feet annually, it requires but an annual average increase of 10 cubic feet per acre to cover such depletion. and this is well within the range of possibility for most of our forest area. If increasing accessibility should further increase the cut, increased efficiency in conservation and reforestation should make it good.*

Represented in the three great forest divisions of Canada are approximately 160 different species of plants reaching tree size. Thirty-one of these species are coniferous, the wood of which forms 80 per cent of our standing timber and 95 per cent of our sawn lumber. Merely to catalogue our merchantable woods is impossible here.

To present an adequate survey of this great national asset it is necessary first to give a general review of operations in the woods, following this by surveys of saw-mill operations and of pulp and paper manufacturing respectively, the two great primary industries founded directly upon the forest. Again, on lumber and paper are founded the long and varied array of our wood and paper-consuming industries.

Operations in the Woods.—The value of the primary products resulting from operations in the forests of Canada is now over $200 millions annually, being made up of logs and bolts for saw-mills valued at over $80 millions; pulpwood for domestic use and export valued at $60 millions; firewood valued at $40 millions; railway ties valued at $14 millions; poles and round mining timber valued at $3 millions each; and other primary forest products, such as square timber, fence posts and rails and wood for distillation. It has been estimated that our total primary forest production involves the cutting of over two and a half billion cubic feet of standing timber annually.

---

*See Chapter II.

A Log Drive on an Eastern River

Lumbering in British Columbia
Photo by Can. Govt. Motion Picture Bureau

The Lumber Industry

	1871	1925
Number of sawmills	6,608	2,700
Employees (number)	38,791	35,458
Wages and salaries ($)	6,321,395	34,097,006
Products ($)	31,148,242	134,413,845

Lumbering first began in the Lower St. Lawrence area and the Maritimes; extended to the Ottawa; thence to Georgian Bay, Rainy River, and the spruce regions north of the Prairies; thence westward to British Columbia. British Columbia now furnishes over one-third of Canada's lumber; fifteen years ago it furnished less than one-fifth. To the pioneer the forest was the central fact of existence, furnishing him with his house and fire but bitterly opposing his plough. Coming at once to the trading era: the first lumber shipped to Europe was during the French *régime* and consisted of masts and spars for the French navy. The historic waney timber trade of which so much has been written centered in Quebec, reaching its height in 1864, when over 1,350 vessels entered that port, carrying away over 20 million cubic feet. When the sawn lumber trade and the deal trade developed the centre shifted to Montreal.

At Confederation, operations in the woods were primitive compared with those carried on by the lumber and pulp companies of to-day, most of the work consisting in the felling of pine and the squaring of timber by hand in the woods, the timbers then being hauled by oxen or horses to the nearest stream, assembled in rafts and floated down to Quebec, where they were loaded on vessels for the United Kingdom. To-day, with the increased costs of longer haulage as the more accessible forests become exhausted, many improvements have been introduced. Logging railways in some cases now transport the logs direct from the woods to the mill; tractors are replacing horses in many cases; and in pulp and paper operations there is a tendency to cut pulpwood throughout the year so as to keep up a steady supply for the mills. In British Columbia the scarcity of drivable streams and the greater size of the logs have resulted in methods differing radically from those of the East. One of the most characteristic of these developments has been the use of cable systems whereby the logs are hauled and assembled by donkey engines.

Except in Nova Scotia, ninety per cent of the forest land is still the property of the Crown—the lumbermen having been granted cutting rights only—and is administered by the various Provincial Departments.

Canada's saw-mills produced in 1925 some 3,888,920 thousand feet board measure of sawn lumber, valued at $99,725,519. The greater part of this lumber was coniferous softwood, as the supply of the more valuable hardwoods such as hickory, oak and walnut (fairly plentiful in southern Ontario and Quebec at the time of Confederation), has been almost exhausted. The mills also produced in 1925 3,161,459 thousand shingles valued at $10,372,736; 1,292,963 thousand lath valued at $6,160,976; 706,700 cords of prepared pulpwood valued at $9,160,976; and 5,041,256 sawn railway ties valued at $3,474,944; as well as large quantities of box shooks, veneer, pickets, staves, hoops and heading, spoolwood and other miscellaneous products; bringing the total value of the products of the industry up to $134,413,845—four times that of Confederation days.

Markets for Canadian lumber at Confederation were largely confined to the United States and Great Britain. They now cover practically all the more important countries of the world, having extended even into the Orient in recent years. There is also a considerable trade in lumber between British Columbia and Eastern Canada *via* the Panama Canal. Though the industry has moved westward, there is a tendency toward consolidation of companies, especially in the matter of timber holdings, and toward the building, in Eastern Canada at least, of fewer and smaller but more efficient sawmills located nearer to the source of supply.

The Pulp and Paper Industry

	1871	1925
Number of mills	21	114
Employees (Number)	760	28,031
Wages ($)	197,815	38,560,905
Products ($)	1,071,651	193,092,937

The pulp and paper industry to-day ranks first among Canadian manufacturing industries in gross and net value of products, as well as in wages and salaries paid. This development has practically all taken place since Confederation, the greater part of it during the present century. In the census of 1871 the mills of this class recorded were all paper mills. Ten years later, in 1881, there were only five pulp mills in operation, with a total capital of only $92,000, 68 employees and an output valued at $63,300. In 1925 the output of the industry in pulp alone was valued at over $100 millions.

The first paper mill in Canada was established in St. Andrews in 1803, and the first Ontario mill was erected at Crooks' Hollow about 1825. At this time and until after Confederation the industry was confined to the manufacture of paper from rags. The supply of raw material, however, was limited, and the manufacturers were soon forced to experiment with other materials. Straw, esparto grass, cotton waste, and fibres from the stems, leaves and other parts of numerous annual plants were tried, but the small proportion of paper-making material recoverable from these sources soon led to experiments in the use of wood. Finally spruce, balsam, fir and hemlock were found to be the most suitable for the manufacture of paper of the average grades, although rags are still used for certain grades.

Under the new conditions, while the older paper mills prepared their own fibre, the rapidly increasing use of wood pulp gave rise to a number of mills which specialized in the manufacture of pulp to supply the needs of the paper makers. What is claimed to be the first wood-pulp mill in Canada was erected by Angus Logan and Co. about 1870 at Windsor Mills in Quebec, where the Canada Paper Co. now operates a pulp and paper mill. In 1887 Charles Riordon installed the first sulphite mill in Canada, at Merritton in the Niagara Peninsula. The sulphate or kraft process of pulp manufacture is a more recent development, the first mill in America being that of the Brompton Pulp and Paper Co. at East Angus, Quebec, which commenced operating in 1907. These developments have resulted in the existence to-day of three classes of mills in the industry: those engaged in the manufacture of pulp only; those making paper only; and combined mills making both pulp and paper. With regard to pulp production the mills altogether in 1925 produced 2,772,507 tons of pulp valued at $100,216,383. Of this, 1,654,549 tons valued at $47,803,623 were used in combined pulp and paper mills for the manufacture of paper; 155,925

A Pulp and Paper Mill
Photo by Can. Govt. Motion Picture Bureau

tons, valued at $6,153,437, were sold to other paper mills in Canada; and 962,033 tons, valued at $46,259,323, were made for the export trade. Of the total quantity of pulp produced, over half was ground-wood, about one quarter was unbleached sulphite, over eight per cent was bleached sulphite and the remainder was sulphate or kraft pulp and screenings.

The total production of paper in 1925 was 1,884,705 tons, which with certain unspecified products was valued at $140,680,177. News-print and similar paper made up 1,536,523 tons, or 81 per cent of the total, valued at $106,268,641. Of the remainder, paper boards made up eight per cent, wrapping paper about five per cent, book and writing paper four per cent, and miscellaneous papers the remaining two per cent. The production of paper has increased by over 120 per cent in the last nine years in Canada, chiefly owing to the increase in the production of newsprint, although practically all the different kinds of paper that are used in Canada at the present time are being pro-duced in Canadian mills. Canada's newsprint production in 1926 was almost 200,000 tons more than that of the United States, hitherto the world's chief producer. This definitely establishes Canada's position as the greatest producer of this commodity in the world.

A striking reflection of the increased production of newsprint is seen in the trade figures. The export trade in paper was non-existent at Con-federation, in fact did not develop until the beginning of the present century, newsprint paper being absent from exports until after 1900. By 1910, however, the exports of newsprint paper were valued at over $2,000,000; in 1920 they were valued at over $53,000,000; whilst during the calendar year 1926 Canada exported 1,731,986 tons of newsprint valued at $114,090,595. This single item of export thus ranks at present second only to wheat. Canada's exports of news-print are probably greater than those of the rest of the world combined. They are more than seven times as great as those of Germany, her nearest competitor, and they exceed those of the eleven other most important exporting countries by over 280,000 tons.

It is interesting further to note that at the time of Confederation the wood group (there being then no paper exported) made up over 41 per cent of the total export trade, amounting to $18 millions out of a total of about $45 millions. To-day the wood and paper group, with an export trade of $286 millions, are but 22 per cent of total exports, though they are still second only to agricultural products. At Confederation, the wood exports were almost entirely of raw or unmanufactured forest products, such as square timber, logs, bolts, etc., the manufactured wooden products representing less than one per cent of the total value of this group. In 1926, however, manufac-tured articles made of wood, including paper and paper goods, formed more than sixty per cent of the total value of the wood and paper group of exports, while unmanufactured forest products made up less than forty per cent. The change is characteristic of the industries which depend on the forest for their raw material. At the time of Confederation, the four provinces were largely "hewers of wood and drawers of water" in this respect for the wood-using industries of the United States and Great Britain. This stage has now been passed, and each year sees a smaller percentage of our saw-logs, pulpwood and other forest products exported in the unmanufactured state. As an example, the exportation of pulpwood has increased but little in late years, though the manufacture has kept pace with the industry at a satisfactory rate, while paper, the finished product of the industry, has shown one of the most remarkable increases in the whole history of trade.

Industries Founded on Lumber and Paper.

In 1871 there were 8,000 establishments depending on saw-mills and paper mills for their raw material. They employed about 27,000 workers and paid them over $6 millions a year in wages, their products being valued at about $20 millions. Among these industries were some that sound strange to our ears in the present day, such as spinning wheel factories, carving and gilding establishments, bellows manufacturers and manufacturers of paper collars. The building of ships, then largely of wood, was carried on in 252 shipyards and gave employment to over 6,000 workers in 1871. As contrasted with this, there were in 1925 only 3,838 establishments of this nature (wood and paper-using industries), but they were of vastly larger scale individually. They gave employment to over 64,000 workers, had a total payroll of over $75 millions, and manufactured products valued at over $100 millions.

The manufacture of silk of a quality in many respects superior to the product of the silk worm, from Canadian spruce wood; the production of linoleum, dynamite, and gramophone records from a flour made of wood; the operation of sawmills having a capacity of over half a million feet board measure in ten hours; the production of newsprint paper in a continuous sheet over twenty feet wide at the rate of over half an acre a minute from a single machine; these are a few of the developments of the forest industries of Canada that could hardly have been foreseen by the Fathers of Confederation.

CHAPTER VIII.—MINING

Mining ranks third among Canada's primary industries, with mineral products becoming more and more a governing factor in commerce and industry. Already a heavy contributor to the world's metal markets, Canada is also phenomenally rich in coal and asbestos. Thirty-five per cent of the freight tonnages moved in Canada are from and to the mines. Particularly notable has been the increase in mining activity during the past three years.

Historical.—It is almost exactly two hundred years since the mining and metallurgical industries of Canada were founded. Operations were at first confined to coal and iron ore, and the manufacture of cast and wrought iron. The coal seams of Cape Breton have the distinction of being the first to be worked in North America (mentioned in a volume by Nicolas Denys published in Paris, 1672). Metallurgy began on the St. Maurice River when in 1730 a furnace for smelting the local bog iron ores was established. The St. Maurice forges continued to operate until 1880. Another historic discovery (1740) was that of a deposit of argentiferous galena (Anse à la Mine) on Lake Temiskaming, one of the oldest known metalliferous deposits in North America—less than ten miles from the fabulously rich silver veins of Cobalt, unknown for another century and a half.

Though isolated discoveries like these continued, systematic prospecting began only in the middle of the nineteenth century with the setting up of the Geological Survey of Canada under Sir William Logan. With a small but enthusiastic band of assistants, many of them explorers whom Logan himself had trained, the herculean task of exploring, mapping and geologically surveying Eastern Canada was begun. In 1863 a comprehensive "Geology of Canada" was issued, which included an examination of the best known mineral occurrences. Thus between 1843 and 1863, may be said to have occurred the real inauguration of the mining industry in eastern Canada, including iron mining in various parts of Ontario and Quebec; the mining of copper ore in the Eastern Townships of Quebec (where the Acton mine was considered for a time the richest copper mine in the world), the washing of alluvial gold on the St. Francis and other tributaries of the St. Lawrence; and the institution of lode-gold mining in Nova Scotia. Meanwhile the Fraser River and Cariboo gold rushes of the 'fifties had founded the colony of British Columbia.

While the work of the Geological Survey thus marked the first important epoch in the history of Canada's mineral industry, the completion in 1885 of the Canadian Pacific railway opened a second chapter of even greater significance. Vast new territories were rendered accessible in which the prospector showed the way to other enterprise. The most important immediate find was made near Sudbury, Ont., 1883, when in blasting a cutting for the railway a body of nickel-copper ore was uncovered which has since made the district world-famous. Similar discoveries occurred later on in British Columbia, where during the 'nineties a remarkable succession of ore-bodies, especially auriferous copper and argentiferous lead-zinc deposits, was located in

A Blast Furnace

Photo by Can. Govt. Motion Picture Bureau

the southeastern section of the province. As transportation facilities were extended, still other ore deposits in different regions were found, the silver of the Cobalt district, discovered in 1903 during the construction of the Temiskaming and Northern Ontario railway, and the extraordinarily rich gold finds at Porcupine and Kirkland Lake being notable examples. Camp has followed camp in these territories, the latest being the copper-gold discoveries at Rouyn, Que., and at Red Lake, Ont. The famous Klondyke rush of 1898 must not be omitted in this rapid enumeration. At the moment Canada has every reason to believe that she is on the threshold of an era in which the contributions to national wealth from mining will be on a scale not known before, and this at a time when the metals play an increasing part in industry.

MINERAL PRODUCTION OF CANADA

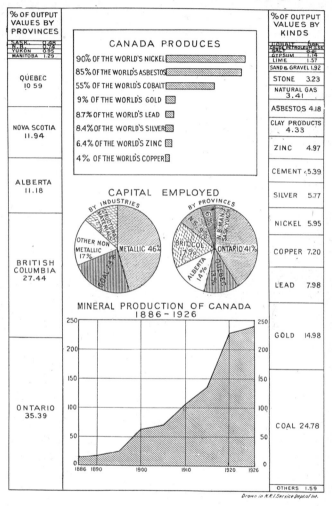

% OF OUTPUT VALUES BY PROVINCES
SASK. 0.46
N.B. 0.74
YUKON 0.95
MANITOBA 1.29
QUEBEC 10.59
NOVA SCOTIA 11.94
ALBERTA 11.18
BRITISH COLUMBIA 27.44
ONTARIO 35.39

CANADA PRODUCES

90% OF THE WORLD'S NICKEL

85% OF THE WORLD'S ASBESTOS

55% OF THE WORLD'S COBALT

9% OF THE WORLD'S GOLD

8.7% OF THE WORLD'S LEAD

8.4% OF THE WORLD'S SILVER

6.4% OF THE WORLD'S ZINC

4% OF THE WORLD'S COPPER

CAPITAL EMPLOYED

BY INDUSTRIES

METALLIC 46%
OTHER NON METALLIC 17%
STRUCTURAL MATERIAL
COAL 22%

BY PROVINCES

ONTARIO 41%
BRIT.COL.
N.S. 9%
ALBERTA 14%
QUEBEC 8.8%
MAN. SASK. YUKON

MINERAL PRODUCTION OF CANADA
1886 - 1926

% OF OUTPUT VALUES BY KINDS
UNSALT
CRUDE PETROLEUM 0.55
SALT 0.81
GYPSUM 1.14
LIME 1.57
SAND & GRAVEL 1.92
STONE 3.23
NATURAL GAS 3.41
ASBESTOS 4.18
CLAY PRODUCTS 4.33
ZINC 4.97
CEMENT 5.39
SILVER 5.77
NICKEL 5.95
COPPER 7.20
LEAD 7.98
GOLD 14.98
COAL 24.78
OTHERS 1.59

Drawn in N.R.I. Service Dept. of Int.

The Modern Industry.—Since 1886, when comprehensive data were first collected for the mining industry as a whole, the advance has been truly remarkable. Valued at $10,221,255 in 1886, or $2.23 per capita, ten years later production had more than doubled, and the per capita value had risen to $4.38. In another ten years, the aggregate had grown three and one-half times, and the per capita

The Great Smelter at Trail, B.C.
Photo by N. R. I. Service

value was $12.81. The total again more than doubled by 1916, when the per capita production reached $22.05. In 1926 Canada's mineral production was computed to be worth $241,245,898, or an average per capita of $25.69. This is the highest point recorded in Canadian history; 1920 being the second highest (at the inflated prices which prevailed) with $227,859,665.

In order of total values the leading mineral products of Canada in 1926 were: coal, $59,797,181; gold, $36,141,891; lead, $19,262,242; copper, $17,386,867; nickel, $14,374,163; silver, $13,934,035; cement, $13,013,283; zinc, $11,996,601; clay products, $10,464,462; asbestos, $10,095,487; natural gas, $8,238,371; stone, $7,807,393; sand and gravel, $4,655,437; lime, $3,790,386; gypsum, $2,761,937; salt, $1,480,-149; crude petroleum, $1,313,730; and cobalt, $1,116,504. This list of 18 products includes all that reached an output value of one million dollars or over; together they made up more than 98 per cent of the total recorded value of mineral production. In addition to these main products, about fifty other minerals were recovered in commercial quantities during the year. Canada's known mineral resources in fact comprise almost every variety of mineral, many of the deposits being sufficiently extensive or rich as to be of world importance. To particularize:—

In 1926 the Dominion produced 90 per cent of the world's supply of nickel, 85 per cent of the world's asbestos, 55 per cent of the world's cobalt, 9 per cent of the world's gold, more than 8 per cent of the world's silver, and about 4 per cent of the world's copper. We lead the world in the production of nickel, cobalt and asbestos; we are third in the output of gold and lead; we hold fourth place among silver-producing countries; and we are the sixth largest producer of aluminium, with every prospect of improving this position when the new smelter at Arvida, Que., comes fully into operation. In the Hollinger gold mine, Canada has one of the greatest gold mines that the world has known, nearly 2 million tons of ore being taken from this mine alone in 1926, while Dome and McIntyre yielded another million tons. The Porcupine and Kirkland Lake areas are in fact among the most important gold camps in the world. The Sullivan mine in British Columbia is likewise the world's largest lead and zinc mine; over a million tons of ore were taken from this mine in 1926. At Trail we have now the world's greatest non-ferrous metallurgical works, treating more than half a million tons of ores and concentrates annually, and producing in 1926 about 262 million pounds of lead, 135 million pounds of zinc, 21 million pounds of copper, 7 million fine ounces of silver, and upwards of 50,000 fine ounces of gold. In coal we have one-sixth of the world's known reserves.

Since 1886 the aggregate value of Canada's mineral output has reached the stupendous sum of $4,013,518,027. For the same period an analysis by groups of mineral products shows:—metallic minerals, 46·0 per cent; fuels and other non-metallic minerals, 37·5 per cent; clay products and other structural materials, 16·5 per cent.

Distribution of mineral production values by provinces for the past 20 years (1907-1926) (during which period the aggregate value of Canada's mineral output was $3,251,362,574) shows the following: Ontario, 39·6 per cent; British Columbia, 22·2 per cent; Nova Scotia, 12·9 per cent; Alberta, 10·9 per cent; Quebec, 9·5 per cent; Yukon, 2·2 per cent; Manitoba, 1·3 per cent; New Brunswick, 0·8 per cent; and Saskatchewan, 0·6 per cent. For the 1926 record see accompanying table.

Mineral Production of Canada by Provinces, 1926

Province	Value of production	Per cent of total
	$	
Nova Scotia	28,792,898	11.94
New Brunswick	1,784,791	0.74
Quebec	25,570,760	10.60
Ontario	85,364,921	35.38
Manitoba	3,127,301	1.30
Saskatchewan	1,146,214	0.47
Alberta	26,962,843	11.18
British Columbia	66,185,780	27.43
Yukon	2,310,390	0.96
Total	241,245,898	100.00

The mining industry in 1926 employed 65,000 workpeople to whom $85,000,000 were distributed in wages. The capital invested was estimated at $640,000,000.

Subsidiary Industries.—On the products of the mine as basis has been reared a most important superstructure of subsidiary industries. Coal and iron are well-known as the basis of industrialism; to these may now be added petroleum. Altogether these industries, (producing iron and its products, the products of the non-ferrous metals,

A Mining Plant in British Columbia

Can. Govt. Motion Picture Bureau

the products of the non-metallic minerals, and chemicals), now produce commodities to the value of approximately $700 millions in a normal year, the capital invested being over $900 millions and the number of employees about 140,000. Included in these manufactures are several of the best known in Canada, such as agricultural implements, machinery, automobiles, electrical apparatus, cement, miscellaneous chemicals, and many others.

Trade.—The exports of Canadian minerals are somewhat under the imports, being $60 millions compared with $96 millions in the last fiscal year, this being accounted for by the heavy imports of coal from the United States. If the manufactures based on the mine are included, an import of $382 millions may be compared with an export of $209 millions.

CHAPTER IX.—THE WATER-POWERS OF CANADA

Water-power is among the chief natural resources of Canada. The physical reason lies in the fact that Canada is estimated to have 142,923 square miles in lakes, an area larger than the whole of the United Kingdom—larger in fact than the fresh water area of any other country in the world. As many of these lakes are situated at a considerable height above sea level, it follows that the rivers generate abundant water-power.

Altogether Canada has 18¼ million horse-power at ordinary minimum stream flow (i.e. throughout the year), rising to over 32 millions for at least six months of the year. Storage basins for regulating the flow would increase this capacity to 41 millions. Of this only about 4½ millions have been harnessed, or less than 11 per cent. Half of the latter development has taken place only during the past ten years, though in the early days the small streams of Ontario, Quebec and the Maritimes played an important part in furnishing power for the flour mills, carding and woollen mills, etc., that were so necessary to the life of a young community.

Compared with other countries, Canada stands second only to the United States in turbine horse-power installation. We also stand second in turbine horse-power installation per 1,000 of population, Norway alone being higher. On a per capita basis Canada has nearly five times the installation of the United States.

The tremendous economic importance of this "white coal" as a source of power is emphasized when it is pointed out that our chief bituminous deposits are in the extreme east and west, Quebec and Ontario having no coal, though they have 60 per cent of the total population and 80 per cent of the manufactures of Canada. The pulp and paper industry, which requires enormous quantities of power, is located for the most part in these provinces. Our power resources, unlike our coal, are very evenly distributed.

In 1925 the central electric stations of Canada generated over 10 billion kilowatt hours. At the very conservative estimate of 2 pounds of coal per kilowatt hour, this was equivalent to 20 million tons of coal (only the most efficient power plants can develop one kilowatt hour per pound of coal), or twice as much coal as is annually imported. The pulp and paper and allied industries generated in the neighbourhood of 2½ billion kilowatt hours, or the equivalent of 5 million tons of coal in energy value. Thus the energy and heat produced by the developed water-powers of Canada is about equal to that of all the coal consumed in Canada for all purposes.

Large hydro-electric development has been possible only since the improvements in long distance transmission of electricity (around 1900), so that at Confederation and for many years after there was nothing of the present vast enterprise. Even in 1900 there was only 170,000 horse-power developed in Canada. By 1905 it had increased to 450,000, or by 165 per cent; by 1910 it had leaped to 975,000 horse-power, and by 1915 to 2,100,000 horse-power During the next ten years this had more than doubled, reaching 4,556,000 in 1926. At Niagara Falls alone $3\frac{1}{4}$ billion kilowatt hours were produced on the Canadian side in 1925. The St. Lawrence with some $2\frac{1}{4}$ million potential horse-power on the international section and about as much again on the section below has hardly been touched; and there are still thousands of potential horse-power in the waters flowing over the falls of the St. John, the Ottawa, the Gatineau, the Lievre, the Nelson and numerous other great rivers.

The age of electricity, as already said, is comparatively young—not older than a quarter of a century—but already there is scarcely a village in Ontario of over 1,000 population not enjoying the advantages of electricity. In British Columbia, for each 100 of the population, $17 \cdot 3$ families are using electricity for lighting their homes; for all Canada the average is $11 \cdot 5$. This means (reckoning $4 \cdot 32$ to a family) that over 50 per cent of the homes in Canada, rural and urban both included, are using electricity for lighting and other domestic purposes. The investment in Canadian central electric power stations in 1925 was $726 millions, nearly double that of 1917, the largest total for any single branch of industry.

Niagara Falls

Can. Govt. Motion Picture Bureau

CHAPTER X.—THE FISHERIES OF CANADA

Production of Fisheries, 1870—$6,600,000
Production of Fisheries, 1925—$48,000,000

The Canadian Fishing Grounds.—Canada's fishing grounds are perhaps the most extensive in the world. On the Atlantic, from Grand Manan to Labrador, the coast line, not including lesser bays and indentations, measures over 5,000 miles. The bay of Fundy, 8,000 square miles in extent, the gulf of St. Lawrence, fully ten times that size, and other ocean waters, comprise not less than 200,000 square miles, or over four-fifths of the area of the fishing grounds of the North Atlantic. In addition, there are 15,000 square miles of Atlantic inshore waters controlled entirely by the Dominion. Large as are these areas they represent only a part of the fishing grounds of Canada. Hudson Bay, with a shore 6,000 miles in length, is larger than the Mediterranean; the Pacific coast of the Dominion measures 7,180 miles in length and is exceptionally well sheltered; whilst throughout the interior is a series of lakes which together contain more than half of the fresh water on the planet, Canada's share of the Great Lakes alone amounting to over 34,000 square miles, a total which does not include lake Winnipeg (9,457 square miles), lake Manitoba, and others of even greater area. The fisheries of Canada are those of a continent rather than of a country.

Still more important than the extent of the Canadian fishing grounds is the quality of their product. It is an axiom among authorities that food fishes improve in proportion to the purity and coldness of the waters in which they are taken. Judged by this standard, the Canadian cod, halibut, herring, mackerel, whitefish and salmon are the peer of any in the world. It is possible, therefore, to state that by far the most valuable fisheries of the western hemisphere, if not of the globe, belong to Canada.

Historical.—Fishing may be regarded as the first industry to be systematically prosecuted by Europeans in what is to-day the Canadian domain. From a date which precedes authentic record, the Normans, the Bretons and the Basques were on the cod-banks of Newfoundland. Cabot, in 1498, when he first sighted the mainland of North America, gave it the name of "Bacalaos," the Basque word for codfish, which he found already in use. Cape Breton, one of the oldest place-names in America, is another memorial of the early French fishermen. The voyages of the early explorers along the coast soon showed that the cod were as plentiful inshore as on the outer banks, and it became

A Salmon Cannery in British Columbia
Can. Govt. Motion Picture Bureau

A Nova Scotia Fish Wharf
Can. Govt. Motion Picture Bureau

common for a crew to anchor in a bay, erect a hut on shore, and make daily excursions to the fishing grounds—the product being salted and dried on land and at the end of the season shipped to France. Soon the fishermen began to stay all winter and thus to erect permanent fishing settlements. Jacques Cartier, when he sailed up the St. Lawrence in 1534, found traces everywhere of these early "Captains Courageous" and their rivalries in arms no less than in the capture of the teeming product which had tempted them so far from home. These quarrels were eventually handed down to recent times in our long-drawn-out controversies with the United States over fishing rights.

The great part played by the fisheries in the early history of Canada was that of providing a much-needed food supply for the settlers. The *rôle* has again been played in recent years by the lake fisheries of the West.

Until the arrival of the Loyalists all other fishing but cod was neglected. Moreover, during the early part of the nineteenth century, only the inshore fisheries were developed. It was not until 1873 that the deep-sea fishing fleet put out from Lunenburg, now the chief centre of the deep-sea fishery.

The Modern Industry.—The existing fishing industry of Canada is the growth of the past half-century. In 1844, the estimated value of the catch was only $125,000. It doubled in the following decade, and by 1860 had well passed the million mark. Ten years later it was

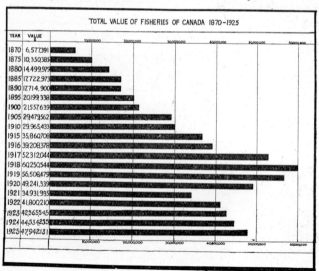

TOTAL VALUE OF FISHERIES OF CANADA 1870-1925

YEAR	VALUE
1870	6,577,391
1875	10,350,385
1880	14,499,979
1885	17,722,973
1890	17,714,900
1895	20,199,338
1900	21,557,639
1905	29,479,562
1910	29,965,433
1915	35,860,708
1916	39,208,378
1917	52,312,044
1918	60,250,544
1919	56,508,479
1920	49,241,339
1921	34,931,935
1922	41,800,210
1923	42,565,545
1924	44,534,235
1925	47,942,131

$6 millions, and this was again more than doubled by 1878. In the 90's it passed $20 millions and in 1911, $34 millions. In 1925, it was nearly $48 millions. The highest record was reached in 1918, with $60 millions. These figures represent the total value of fish marketed, whether in a fresh, dried, canned or otherwise prepared state.

The above extraordinary expansion reflects numerous changes in conditions. In Confederation days the cod and haddock of the Atlantic were the most important items of the catch; to-day British Columbia, with her enormous salmon and halibut fisheries, takes the lead amongst the provinces (a leadership that in earlier times belonged to Nova Scotia), accounting for nearly half of the entire catch. The lobster fishery of the East has also become vastly more important, until it is now the largest fishery of the kind in the world. But the greatest element of change has been contributed by improvements in the methods of catching and preparing the fish, and especially by the development of the fish-canning industry. In 1870, there were but three lobster canneries on the Atlantic coast of Canada; to-day, these canneries number about 500, giving work to nearly 7,000 people, and 30,000,000 lobsters is a normal catch. The salmon canneries of the Pacific, which are all large ones, now number 69; these figures are ten times as large as they were when the first shipment of canned salmon went from British Columbia to Great Britain around the Horn.

From the standpoint of capital and labour, the fisheries are of considerable importance. In the primary operations of catching the fish, the total capital represented by vessels, boats, nets, traps, piers, wharves, etc., is about $25 millions, of which $21 millions are invested in the sea fisheries and over $4 millions in the inland fisheries. Employees in these primary operations number 58,000. In the secondary operations of fish-canning and curing (the establishments number about 850) the capital invested is about $21 million, whilst the employees number about 16,000, including 6,500 females.

Value of Fisheries by Provinces, 1870, 1900 and 1925

Province	Value of production			Per cent from each province		
	1870	1900	1925	1870	1900	1925
	$	$	$	p.c.	p.c.	p.c.
Prince Edward Island ..	–	1,059,193	1,598,119	–	4·9	3·3
Nova Scotia............	4,019,425	7,809,152	10,213,779	61·1	36·2	21·3
New Brunswick.........	1,131,433	3,769,742	4,798,589	17·2	17·5	10·0
Quebec.................	1,161,551	1,989,279	3,044,919	17·7	9·2	6·3
Ontario................	264,982	1,333,294	3,436,412	4·0	6·2	7·2
Manitoba..............	–	718,159	1,466,939	–	3·3	3·1
Saskatchewan..........	–		494,882	–		1·0
Alberta...............	–		458,504	–		1·0
British Columbia.......	–	4,878,820	22,414,618	–	22·7	46·8
Yukon Territory.......	–	–	15,370	–	–	0·0
Total..........	6,577,391	21,557,639	47,942,131	100·0	100·0	100·0

Fisheries Production by Principal Kinds, 1925. Each over $1,000,000 in value

Kind		Quantity	Value
			$
Salmon	cwt.	1,933,260	15,760,630
Cod	"	2,309,000	6,232,821
Lobsters	"	340,838	5,552,977
Halibut	"	340,007	4,185,391
Herring	"	2,413,973	3,117,841
Whitefish	"	186,648	1,990,108
Haddock	"	344,386	1,171,555
Trout	"	81,292	1,097,728
Pickerel or doré	"	86,877	1,056,169
Smelts	"	76,795	1,035,504
Sardines	bbl.	158,533	1,017,206

Trade.—The domestic consumption of fish is relatively small in Canada (it is estimated at 22 pounds per capita) and the trade depends largely upon foreign markets. Perhaps 60 per cent of the annual catch is an average export, of which the United States takes approximately one-third, and Great Britain one-fifth. In the fiscal year 1926, total exports amounted to $37,487,517, of which $14,115,596 went to the United States and $7,264,516 to Great Britain. The most important single export is canned salmon (to Great Britain and European markets), followed closely by cod, dry salted (to the West Indies, South America, etc.). For fresh fish, especially whitefish and lobsters, the United States is the chief market. In brief, Canada's export trade in fish falls below that of Great Britain and Norway alone; including Newfoundland it exceeds both. Canadian imports of fish in 1926, amounted to $2,590,515.

Game Fish.—The above is a purely industrial and commercial survey. Fishing for sport, however, has its economic side in a country of such famous game fish as the salmon of the Restigouche, the black bass of the Quebec and Ontario highlands and the trout of the Nipigon. A considerable public revenue is derived from the leasing of waters in sparsely settled districts to clubs and individuals for sporting purposes. Several hundreds of guides find employment here during the summer months.

The Government and the Fisheries.—A large staff of inspectors, overseers and guardians is employed by the Government to enforce the fishery laws. The expenditure of the Dominion on the fisheries in the fiscal year 1926 was $1,560,166 and its revenue $264,546. The main object has been the prevention of depletion, the enforcement of close seasons, the forbidding of obstructions and pollutions, and the regulation of nets, gear and of fishing operations generally. In addition, an extensive system of fish culture has been organized, while stations for the conduct of biological research into the numerous complex problems furnished by the fisheries are established at St. Andrews, N.B., and Nanaimo, B.C. The Government has also from time to time rendered direct assistance in specific cases of difficulty. Finally, a fleet of armed cruisers patrols the coastal and inland waters for the prevention of poaching and the enforcement of regulations. There are efficient Fisheries Branches under most of the Provincial Governments.

CHAPTER XI.—THE FUR TRADE

The fur trade has played a most important part in the history of Canada. From the earliest times the fisherman upon the "banks" had traded in furs; as the demand in France and Europe increased, adventurers came for the fur trade exclusively. Later, when the whole movement widened, the French government granted monopolies of the trade on condition that a certain number of settlers should be brought out each year. Pont Gravé and Chauvin built Tadoussac in 1599 as a centre for the fur trade with the Indians of the Saguenay; when routes were discovered further inland the founding of Quebec and Montreal followed. The trade spread west and south, convoys bringing the furs yearly to Montreal and Quebec. "Beaver" became the Canadian currency—a significant incident.

The first expedition to Canada financed by English capital was in response to the lure of the fur trade; it voyaged to Hudson Bay about the year 1662. This venture was instigated by Radisson and Groseilliers, two French *coureurs de bois* who had travelled in the rich fur country north of Lake Superior, had sought to rouse interest in France, but being repulsed turned to England. The charter of the "Adventurers of England Trading into Hudson's Bay" followed in 1670, Prince Rupert becoming the first governor of "The Great Company".

After the Seven Years War, about 1771, commenced a period of intense competition among the fur traders, now swollen to an army. Some years later (1783-4) several of these joined hands and formed a new company chartered as the "North West Company". The competition between the new organization and the Hudson Bay Company was quite as keen as before, but in 1821, after many years of strife, the two were finally joined under the name of the older company. In 1869 the Company surrendered its quasi-governmental functions to Canada, in consideration of extensive grants, and became a trading concern pure and simple. It may be said with truth that the fur trade occupied and held the great western domain of the Dominion till such time as settled government became feasible, and for this it must always receive due recognition.

The Modern Industry.—The fur trade is still one of Canada's notable assets, and a growing one, notwithstanding that the progress of settlement and improved methods of capture are driving the animals further and further afield and leading to the use of many species once rejected. Early records are vague. In 1667 exports of furs to France and the West Indies were valued at only 550 francs.

84

Even in 1850 the value of furs exported was but £19,395 ($93,872). In 1880 the value of pelts taken was given as $987,555. In 1910 this had become $1,927,550; in 1920-21, $10,151,594; and in 1925-26, the latest production return, close upon 15 millions. For 1926 the exports were valued at $17,017,501. Muskrat has now replaced beaver as the most valuable peltry, with mink, fox and sable following. Canadian manufactures of fur goods and the home consumption are annually increasing, with the growth of wealth and population. When settlement has planted its furthest northern outpost in Canada, the area which will continue to yield the historic peltries will still have to be reckoned in hundreds of thousands of square miles. It is the function of the fur trade to turn this vast domain—so often hastily reckoned as waste—to perpetual economic use.

During the Great War the fur market of the world, long centered in London, changed to the United States. In 1914, of the $5,100,000 worth of undressed furs exported from Canada to England and the United States, England received $3,000,000; in 1919 out of $13,300,000 worth thus exported only $3,700,000 went to England. Recently, however, the English market is again taking a large proportion of Canada's exports of raw furs, the latest figures showing that of the undressed furs exported to England and the United States, $6,435,715 worth went to the former and $10,319,264 worth to the latter. One result or concomitant of the changed situation is of special concern to Canada: At the close of the war Montreal became an international

"Donalda"—First Prize Dark Silver Adult Female Fox

fur market, holding the first fur auction sale to take place in Canada in 1920, when 949,565 pelts, valued at $5,057,114, were sold. Auction sales are also now held at Winnipeg and Edmonton. The Canadian fur market is now firmly established, sales being held three and four times annually.

Conservation.—The conservation of the wild life of Canada became a special object of government policy through the organization in 1916 of the Advisory Board on Wild Life Protection, to co-ordinate the efforts of various departments and branches of the Dominion Government. The Northwest Game Act and the Migratory Birds Convention Act are the most important legislation in the field in which the Board operates and upon which it makes advisory recommendations. The Board also investigates and studies all problems relating to the protection and better utilization of fur-bearing animals, "big game" mammals, and bird life, whether game birds, insectivorous birds or others.

Fur Farming.—Even in the early days of the fur trade it was the practice for trappers to keep foxes caught in warm weather alive until the fur was prime; from this practice has arisen the modern industry of fur farming. The industry is devoted chiefly to the raising of the silver fox, a colour phase of the common red fox established through experiments in breeding carried on by the pioneer fox farmers. There are now in Canada 2,130 fox farms with a total of 42,125 silver foxes, 1,736 patch or cross foxes, 1,196 red foxes and 735 blue foxes. There are also 210 farms raising fur-bearing animals other than foxes, chief among which are mink, raccoon, skunk and muskrat. The value of fur-bearing animals on farms in 1925 was $9,898,019, the value of those sold off in that year being $2,897,270. In addition the value of pelts sold from fur farms in 1925 was $781,383, this representing about four per cent of the total value of the fur production of Canada in that year.

CHAPTER XII.—THE MANUFACTURES OF CANADA

Value of Manufactures, 1870—$221 millions
Value of Manufactures, 1925—$2,948 millions
Employees in Manufactures, 1870—188,000
Employees in Manufactures, 1925—544,000

At Confederation Canadian manufactures were still in their infancy. In primitive societies (as among the early settlers of Canada in the 17th and 18th centuries) manufacturing is normally carried on within the household for the needs of the household. At a later period, small shops spring up to meet demands of the immediate neighbourhood. Still later, with the invention of power-driven machinery and the cheapening of transportation (the so-called "Industrial Revolution") the factory system is born, and manufacturing becomes concentrated in large establishments situated usually in industrial centres of considerable size.

This last-mentioned stage of development was no more than well founded in Canada in 1867. Flour-milling, it is true, had reached considerable proportions, and there were substantial clothing and iron and steel manufactures. All told, however, the value of Canadian manufactured products in 1870, as recorded at the first Dominion census, reached only $221 millions, the capital invested in factories being $78 millions, and the number of employees 188,000.

The encouragement of Canadian manufactures by tariffs had been discussed during the '50's and to some extent commenced in 1858, but it was not until 1878 that a general policy of protection was adopted. Thereafter, a considerable growth took place, though at the end of the nineteenth century the value of products was only $481 millions, the capital employed $446 millions, and the number of employees 339,000.

It is the present century, however, that has witnessed the chief forward movement in Canadian manufactures, the result of two great influences, first, the "boom" accompanying the opening up of the "last best West", which greatly increased the demand for manufactured goods of all kinds and especially construction materials, and secondly, the war, which not only created enormous new demands but left a permanent imprint upon the variety and efficiency of Canadian plants. In 1910, when the first of these influences was but partly felt, the value of Canadian manufactures had risen to $1,165 millions, the capital invested to $1,247 millions, and the number of employees to 515,000; but by 1920, the "peak" year, the gross value of Canadian

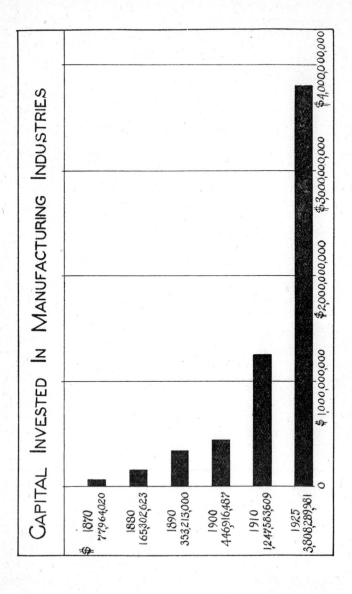

manufactured products was no less than \$3,772 millions, the capital invested \$3,371 millions, and the number of employees 609,586. Hundreds of millions of capital had been attracted from outside in the achieving of this striking result. The figures have declined somewhat since, but the accompanying table will reveal the situation by provinces in the latest year for which the data are available (1925).

Province	Number of establishments	Capital	Number of employees	Value of Products	
				$	Per cent of Total
Prince Edward Island.......	318	2,576,677	2,317	4,290,149	0.15
Nova Scotia................	1,184	117,326,491	16,529	65,033,701	2.20
New Brunswick............	861	91,509,933	17,275	73,374,660	2.49
Quebec....................	6,995	1,136,033,133	168,237	820,563,757	27.82
Ontario...................	9,386	1,925,593,482	262,307	1,527,154,660	51.79
Manitoba..................	769	120,342,238	20,027	124,145,763	4.21
Saskatchewan..............	650	31,607,896	4,405	40,093,273	1.36
Alberta...................	734	69,805,848	9,366	75,113,517	2.56
British Columbia........... Yukon....................	1,434	313,494,283	43,551	218,775,835	7.42
Canada..............	22,331	3,808,289,981	544,014	2,948,545,315	100.00

It will be seen that from Confederation until the present the growth of manufacturing has been between 12 and 15 times. Some of the outstanding features of this progress are shown below:—

Industries	1870	1925
	$	$
Flour and grist mill products.................................	39,135,919	187,944,731
Pulp and paper mills..	1,071,651	193,092,937
Saw-mills.	31,148,242	134,413,845
Slaughtering and meat-packing...............................	3,799,552	163,816,810
Butter and cheese...	1,601,738	124,828,754
Electric light and power.....................................	–	102,587,882
Automobiles..	–	110,835,380
Cotton yarn and cloth.......................................	781,800	72,781,517
Sugar refineries...	4,132,750	68,445,879
Rubber goods (including footwear)...........................	502,615	78,229,574
Castings and forgings..	7,325,531	61,754,339
Electrical apparatus and supplies.............................	–	60,158,837

A summary of the existing industry is worthy of a paragraph. According to the latest census available, Canada possessed in 1925 22,331 manufacturing establishments, whose capital investment in lands, buildings, equipment, etc., amounted to \$3,808,289,981, which employed 544,014 persons with salaries and wages amounting to \$596,015,171, consumed \$1,587,665,408 worth of raw materials (not including fuel) and produced goods to the value of \$2,948,545,315.

The leading centres of manufactures to-day are Montreal and Toronto, with totals of $459 millions and $409 millions, respectively. After these come Hamilton with $141 millions, Vancouver with $71 millions, Winnipeg with $70 millions, Oshawa with $43 millions, and Ottawa with $40 millions. There are 25 other places having manufactures of $10 millions or over.

The twenty-five leading industries of to-day are also tabulated herewith, one of the most interesting of recent developments being the forging of pulp and paper to first place, a position long held by flour-milling, with slaughtering and meat-packing and saw-milling next in order.

Statistics of Twenty-five Leading Industries of Canada, 1925

Industries	Number of employees	Capital	Value of products
	No.	$	$
Pulp and paper	28,031	460,397,772	193,092,937
Flour and grist-mill products	6,166	60,104,258	187,944,731
Slaughtering and meat-packing	10,709	54,316,043	163,816,810
Saw-mills	35,458	204,134,003	134,413,845
Butter and cheese	10,548	37,292,100	124,828,754
Automobiles	10,301	74,678,451	110,835,380
Electric light and power	13,263	726,721,087	102,587,882
Rubber goods including footwear	12,962	65,562,734	78,229,574
Cotton yarn and cloth	20,497	83,610,686	72,781,517
Sugar refineries	2,784	50,089,717	68,445,879
Castings and forgings	17,120	84,812,441	61,754,339
Bread and other bakery products	12,438	33,810,501	60,392,439
Electrical apparatus and supplies	14,112	75,375,623	60,158,837
Non-ferrous metal smelting	5,104	61,691,928	56,633,793
Printing and publishing	14,187	48,399,803	53,886,802
Railway rolling stock	20,202	78,039,179	53,050,665
Petroleum	3,738	50,580,549	50,762,127
Hosiery, knit goods and gloves	14,698	49,350,474	48,555,434
Clothing, women's factory	13,490	21,704,956	46,779,771
Biscuits, confectionery and chewing gum	11,958	40,770,096	46,745,355
Cigars and cigarettes	5,846	30,563,901	41,985,554
Boots and shoes, leather	13,791	30,863,482	40,022,515
Planing mills, sash and door factories	10,105	48,743,683	40,009,152
Breweries	4,073	51,222,456	38,897,995
Clothing, men's factory	10,818	24,180,348	38,236,384

That Canada with her vast agricultural, forest and other resources should be the centre of large flour-milling, meat-packing, butter and cheese, fish-packing, lumber, pulp and paper, and electric power industries is natural enough. In an allied category stand a number of industries such as tanning and leather, brewing and distilling, biscuits and confectionery, chemical, etc. But there are also a large number of industries based on imported raw materials which have attained to very considerable proportions; such as cotton and woollen textiles, rubber goods, sugar, automobiles, all of which are now playing a

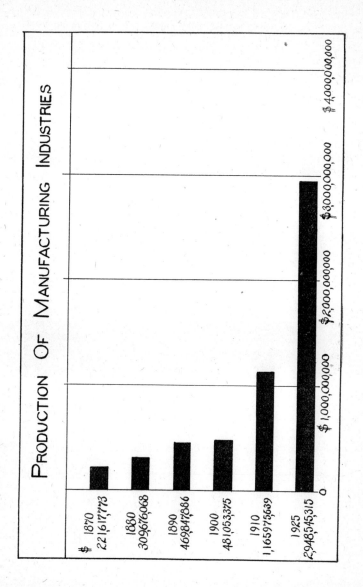

PRODUCTION OF MANUFACTURING INDUSTRIES

$ 1870
221,617,773

1880
309,676,068

1890
469,847,886

1900
481,053,375

1910
1,165,975,639

1925
2,948,545,315

$1,000,000,000

$2,000,000,000

$3,000,000,000

$4,000,000,000

substantial part in the industrial life of the Dominion, ranking as will be seen in the accompanying table among the leading manufacturing industries.

Trade in Manufactures.—At Confederation the main objective of Canadian manufactures was the supply of the local or home market, though certain industries, such as flour and lumber, had looked to the foreign market from a very early period. Gradually, however, the territory served by Canadian manufactures has expanded, until to-day we are sending manufactured goods to virtually every country in the world. Since the beginning of the present century alone the exports of Canadian manufactured goods have gone up from $99 millions to $695 millions. To assist this attack upon world markets a Commercial Intelligence Service has been established in the Department of Trade and Commerce which now has commissioners or trade representatives at 26 strategic points in other countries. Meanwhile, the home market has been cultivated, though from the nature of things many classes of manufactures are imported. Very significant in this connection, however, is the fact that in recent years Canada's exports of manufactures have been larger than her imports.

A Canadian Agricultural Implement Factory

Courtesy of Royal Bank

CHAPTER XIII.—CONSTRUCTION

In a country which, like Canada, is still in process of development, the building industry occupies a position of high relative importance, the new values thus created often ranking as one of the chief determining factors in current economic progress. Conditions in this respect vary, of course, from year to year; moreover, different phases tend to become specially prominent at different periods.

Railroad construction, for example, saw its period of greatest activity in Canada during the first decade and a half of the present century, when two entirely new transcontinental systems were built and placed in operation. But though incidents of this extraordinary kind occur only at wide intervals, a considerable amount of new trackage is laid annually. In 1925 there were 506 miles of new railway lines opened, 166 miles completed but not opened for traffic, and 559 miles projected or under construction, the net increase in single track mileage being 291 miles. The expenditures of steam and electric railways on maintenance of way and structures account is also a constant item, amounting to $170 or $180 millions. Altogether, investments on new railway trackage and other structures in 1924 were over $48 millions and in 1923 over $68 millions.

Second only to railway building has been the good roads programme of the Dominion and Provincial Governments, undertaken largely since the war. Under the Canada Highways Act, 1919, there has been spent $18,429,107 by the Federal Government; as this was but 40 per cent of the total, the entire expenditure on highways under this Act during the past seven years has been at least $46,000,000. In addition, there have been very heavy expenditures by the provinces, counties, townships and urban municipalities on roads not receiving Dominion aid.

On public utilities in general the annual expenditures on new construction account are often considerable. In this category are included new telegraph and telephone lines, canals, harbours, central electric stations, waterworks, etc. Telephone construction and betterments alone vie with those of the railways.

On building proper, i.e., for houses, factories, business premises, etc., a comprehensive record is difficult to obtain in view of the widespread nature of the operations. An estimate of the more important contracts awarded, however, places the total in the neighbourhood of $300 millions annually. Confirmation of this in part is afforded by the official records of building permits issued in some 60 cities of Canada; in 1926, the value of buildings thus authorized was in the neighbourhood of $156 millions.

In its entirety the building industry in Canada probably represents the expenditure of half a billion dollars in a year of normal activity. This is many times the scale of such operations when the Dominion was first formed.

CHAPTER XIV.—THE TRADE OF CANADA

Trade of Canada, 1868—$120 millions
Trade of Canada, 1927—$2,298 millions

The trade of Canada reflects, as perhaps no other single medium, the growth in the productive system described in the preceding chapters. It represents on the whole a relative expansion and development during the sixty years that has not been surpassed in any other country. From an isolated and dependent community, we have become a nation trading with the ends of the earth, exceeding many of the oldest and largest countries in trade standing. Thus, in volume of trade Canada now stands fifth among the nations (both in exports and imports), only Great Britain, the United States, Germany and France being larger, while in per capita trade we stand second (both exports and imports), being exceeded only by the sister Dominion of New Zealand. Our favourable trade balance per capita was last year the largest in the world. In no other field is the progress of Canada more significantly written than in her trade annals.

Total Trade

Canada's total trade with all countries for the fiscal year 1926 amounted to $2,256,029,000, or about twenty times what it was at Confederation, viz., $119,792,000. At the beginning of the present century it was only about three times as great, total trade in 1900 amounting to $355,889,000. The United States had a population of 75,000,000 before their total foreign trade was as large as that of Canada today.

Total Dominion trade with the United Kingdom in 1868 was $55,522,000, whereas in 1926 it was $672,997,000, or twelve times as great. In 1900, it was only about three times that of 1868. With the United States from Confederation to 1926 our trade increased from $48,010,000 to $1,095,672,000, or twenty-two and one-half times, mostly since 1900 when it was only a trifle more than three times that of 1868.

An analysis of the physical volume of Canada's foreign trade shows that it was greater for both imports and exports in 1926 than for any other year in our history. Statistics have been compiled for the

95

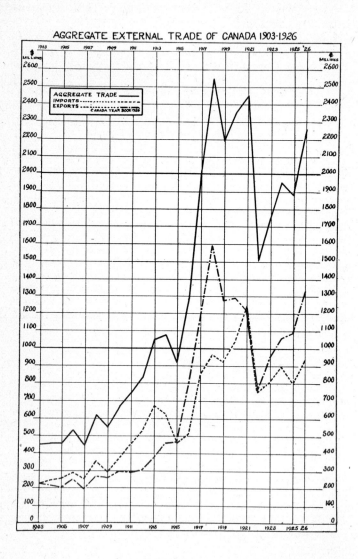

AGGREGATE EXTERNAL TRADE OF CANADA 1903-1926

fiscal years 1921 to 1926, based on 1914 average values, (i.e., eliminating the effects of subsequent changes in prices), as follows:—

Fiscal years	Imports		Exports (Canadian)	
	Declared values	Based on 1914 average values	Declared values	Based on 1914 average values
	$	$	$	$
1914	619,194,000	619,194,000	431,589,000	431,589,000
1921	1,240,159,000	611,286,000	1,189,163,000	543,224,000
1922	747,804,000	505,128,000	740,241,000	497,546,000
1923	802,579,000	592,952,000	931,451,000	692,871,000
1924	893,367,000	637,893,000	1,045,351,000	801,452,000
1925	796,933,000	597,298,000	1,069,067,000	762,941,000
1926	927,403,000	703,875,000	1,315,193,000	897,208,000

The development of a country industrially is often illustrated in the character of the goods it imports and exports. In the early years, Canadian imports consisted chiefly of manufactured products and the exports of raw and semi-manufactured products, but since the opening of the twentieth century the reverse is the rule, a large percentage of the imports consisting of raw and semi-manufactured products for use in Canadian manufacturing industries, while the exports are made up largely of products which have undergone some process of manufacture.

C.P.R. Pier, with Ocean Steamer, Vancouver

N.R.I. Service

Imports

From Confederation to 1926 our total imports from all countries increased from $67,090,000 to $927,329,000, or about fourteen times. The increase from Confederation to 1900 was $105,562,000, or 157 per cent, while from 1900 to 1926 it amounted to $754,677,000, or 437 per cent.

Imports from the United Kingdom amounted at Confederation to $37,617,000, while in 1926 they amounted to $163,731,000, being about four and one-third times greater. From 1868 to 1900 these imports increased $6,663,000 or 18 per cent; from 1900 to 1926 they increased $119,451,000 or 270 per cent.

Canada's imports from the United States at Confederation were valued at $22,660,000, and in 1926 at $609,720,000, being some twenty-seven times greater than in 1868, while in 1900 they were only four and one-half times greater.

Thus in 1868, 90 per cent of Canada's imports were supplied by the United Kingdom and the United States, the proportion from the United Kingdom being 56·1 per cent, and from the United States 33·8 per cent. In 1926, 83 per cent of Canada's total imports came from the United Kingdom and the United States, the proportion from the United Kingdom falling to 17·6 per cent, and that from the United States rising to 65·7 per cent. There has meanwhile been a gradual rise in the percentage of imports from countries other than the United Kingdom and the United States, the proportion in 1868 amounting to 10·1

The Harbour of Montreal

Can. Govt. Motion Picture Bureau

per cent, and in 1926 to 16·7 per cent. In 1868 the 10·1 per cent represented an import value of only \$6,813,000; in 1926 the value was \$153,879,000. Of the latter amount Europe (except the United Kingdom) supplied \$59,700,000; North America (except the United States), \$34,900,000; South America \$17,100,000; Asia \$32,700,000; Oceania \$8,700,000; and Africa \$800,000. In 1868 Canada drew her supplies from a very limited number of countries, but to-day she obtains them from practically every country of the world. The list of the latter includes over 100, British countries numbering about 30 and foreign countries about 70.

An especially important feature as already hinted, is the constantly increasing import into Canada from year to year of raw and semi-manufactured materials, reflecting the ever increasing scope of our manufacturing processes. The following statistics of these imports are of significance as reflecting the expansion in Canadian manufacturing since 1880:—

Commodities		1880	1900	1926
Bituminous coal......................	ton	457,049	2,769,938	13,377,204
Cocoa, raw...........................	lb.	96,983	779,050	16,599,600
Cotton, raw...........................	"	13,237,168	54,912,849	128,560,963
Furs, raw.............................	\$	235,643	1,240,589	8,270,899
Hides, raw............................	\$	1,752,426	4,214,412	9,329,543
Lumber, sawn, or dressed on one side only............................M ft		4,421	99,711	135,045
Manila and sisal grass................	lb.	56,700	....	43,969,900
Rubber, raw..........................	"	264,838	3,002,576	46,986,814
Silk, raw.............................	"	12,928	69,832	529,446
Sugar, raw...........................	"	87,094,176	267,623,607	1,158,544,069
Tin block, ingots etc	"	1,332,000	2,244,100	4,440,900
Tinned plates........................	"	9,795,900	50,210,800	160,203,800
Wool, raw............................	"	7,870,118	8,054,699	13,434,426

Exports

Canada's export trade shows a much greater relative expansion than her import trade in the sixty years that have passed since Confederation. The grand total exports of domestic produce to all countries in 1926 amounted to \$1,315,356,000, which is twenty-seven times larger than the similar exports at Confederation, viz.: \$48,505,000. This again has been largely achieved in the present century. From Confederation to 1900 domestic exports increased \$120,467,000, or 248 per cent, while from 1900 to 1926 they increased \$1,146,384,000, or 678 per cent.

To the United Kingdom, Canadian exports, which at Confederation amounted to \$17,906,000, had increased in 1926 to \$508,238,000, or some twenty-eight times. From Confederation to 1900 the increase was \$78,657,000, or 439 per cent, while from 1900 to 1926 it was \$411,-674,000, or 426 per cent.

Canada's domestic exports to the United States at Confederation were valued at $25,350,000, and in 1926 at $474,987,000, being in 1926 about nineteen times greater than in 1868. In 1900 they were valued at $57,996,000. The increase from 1868 to 1900 was $32,646,000, or 127 per cent, while from 1900 to 1926 it was $416,991,000, or 720 per cent.

In 1868 the exports to the United Kingdom and the United States combined were 89·2 per cent of the total for domestic produce, the proportion for the United Kingdom being 36·9 per cent, and for the United States 52·3 per cent. For the year 1926 the domestic exports of Canada to the United Kingdom and the United States totalled only 74·7 per cent; the proportion for the United Kingdom being 38·6 per cent, and for the United States only 36·1 per cent. The proportion of domestic exports to other countries than the United Kingdom and the United States in 1868 was 10·8 per cent; in 1900 it had dropped to 8·7 per cent, but by 1926 it had risen to 25·3 per cent. This increase was made up from the decline just mentioned in the proportion exported to the United States. At Confederation exports to other countries than the United Kingdom and the United States represented a value of $5,249,000; in 1900 this was $14,413,000, while in 1926 it was $332,131,000, a gain between 1868 and 1900 of $9,164,000 or 174 per cent, and between 1900 and 1926 of $317,718,000 or 2,204 per cent. During the year 1926 our exports by Continents were as

Saint John Harbour, N.B.

N.R.I. Service

follows: Europe (except United Kingdom) $140,300,000; North America (except United States), $41,300,000; South America, $27,400,000; Asia, $77,200,000; Oceania, $32,600,000; and Africa, $13,300,000. Thus, while in 1868 Canadian products reached a very limited number of countries, to-day they find their way into every country of the world. Canada to-day sells her products to more than 113 countries; British countries buying goods from Canada number some 32, and foreign countries some 81. Some significant export records are appended (commodities arranged according to their importance, 1926).

Commodities	1868	1900	1926
	$	$	$
Wheat..	3,648,000	11,995,000	364,201,000
Paper..(1890)	122	30,000	110,105,000
Wheat flour............................(1869)	1,949,000	3,105,000	69,688,000
Planks and boards........................	10,876,000	22,016,000	66,824,000
Wood pulp............................(1890)	168,000	1,816,000	49,910,000
Meats..	1,229,000	13,616,000	37,112,000
Fish..	3,246,000	10,563,000	36,531,000
Automobiles................................		(1906) 63,000	35,717,000
Cheese................................(1869)	550,000	19,856,000	33,719,000
Gold, raw................................	16,000	14,149,000	25,968,000
Oats..	755,000	2,143,000	24,238,000
Barley..	3,187,000	1,010,000	23,182,000
Sugar, refined........................(1879)	1,400	2,000	19,981,000
Cattle..	1,100,000	9,081,000	18,081,000
Furs, undressed............................	434,000	2,265,000	17,198,000
Whiskey..	5,000	397,000	15,712,000
Tires, rubber................................		(1917) 727,000	14,004,000
Copper ore and blister....................	394,000	1,387,000	13,946,000
Lead..	3,000	689,000	13,928,000
Farm implements....................(1878)	86,000	1,692,000	13,628,000
Pulp wood............................(1890)	80,000	903,000	13,056,000
Flaxseed..	77,000	342	12,883,000
Nickel................................(1891)	240,000	1,040,000	12,829,000
Silver................................(1871)	595,000	1,354,000	12,366,000
Laths, palings and pickets..............	144,000	532,000	11,266,000
Asbestos, raw........................(1888)	228,000	491,000	9,921,000

Trade Balances.

From Confederation to 1926, exports to all countries have exceeded imports on twenty-three occasions, while imports have exceeded exports on thirty-six occasions. The excess of exports over imports during the past fifty-nine years has amounted to $1,337,941,000. The largest excess of exports over imports totalled $622,637,000, viz.: during the war year 1918, while the largest excess of imports over exports occurred in the year 1913 and amounted to $294,139,000. The "unfavourable" balances occur in years of heavy capital imports, notably in 1903-1913. The "favourable" balances of the past three years (reaching $401 millions in the fiscal year ended March 31, 1926) no doubt chiefly represent Canada's successful meeting of charges on her war and other obligations abroad. How the present calendar year (1926) record compares with other countries is shown as follows:—

Countries	"Favourable" balance	"Unfavourable" balance
	$	$
United States	377,575,000	
British India	323,895,000	
Canada	275,597,000	
France	646,000	
Germany		31,630,000
United Kingdom		2,264,973,000

Tariff Legislation.—Canada was the first of the British Dominions to grant a trade preference to the produce and manufactures of the United Kingdom and reciprocating British Dominions and Possessions —one of 12½ per cent from April, 1897. In 1898, the preference to Great Britain was increased to 25 per cent, and in 1900 to 33⅓ per cent. To-day it is applicable to practically every British Dominion and possession, except Newfoundland, to whom, however, Canada grants free trade in fish and fish products. When the British preference was enacted in 1897, Canada's imports from the United Kingdom amounted to only $29,401,000, being $8,216,000 or 22 per cent less than at Confederation; from 1897 to 1926 the increase has been 457 per cent.

It was also enacted in the Customs Tariff Act, 1907 (which provided a tripartite tariff scale, viz., the British Preference, the Intermediate and the General), that the Government can, by Order-in-Council, extend the provisions of the Intermediate Tariff in whole or in part to any foreign country that grants equivalent treatment to Canada. Prior to 1906 Canada had no bargaining machinery of the kind. To-day we have trade treaties or agreements with Belgium, Czecho-Slovakia, Finland, France, Japan, Italy, and the Netherlands, whilst in 1925 the provisions of the Intermediate tariff were extended to Spain. By "most favoured nation" provisions in certain British treaties, goods of the following countries get the benefits of the French and Italian treaties when imported into Canada, and Canadian goods get various tariff concessions in those countries, viz.:—

France	Italian Possessions
Colombia	Argentine Republic
Norway	Denmark
Switzerland	Russia
The United Kingdom	Sweden
Italy	Venezuela
British Dominions and	Finland
Possessions	Czecho-Slovakia
French Possessions	

Economic Union of Belgium and Luxembourg and Possessions
The Netherlands and Possessions.

CHAPTER XV.—TRANSPORTATION AND COMMUNICATIONS

The Dominion is a land of magnificent distances. From coast to coast it stretches over 3,500 miles in length, the population, being distributed in the main only along the southern border. Between different parts of the country intervene sections of rough and difficult terrain which present crucial problems both for the transportation engineer and operator. In the pioneer days when the rivers afforded almost the sole routes of travel (the St. Lawrence in particular reaching into the heart of the Continent), difficulties of the same nature were encountered in the frequent falls and rapids. It is significant, therefore, that the earliest important expenditure for public works in Canada was for canals; that later when the railway era began, it was a railway that set the seal to Confederation and another that conditioned the entrance of our westernmost province; and that to-day the two great railway systems are the largest single employers of labour in the Dominion. The periods of rapid railway development, namely in the 'fifties, in the 'eighties and in the first fifteen years of the present century, were attended with the most profound results on general economic conditions in Canada.

The first Canadian railway was constructed in 1836 between St. Johns, Que., and Laprairie; it was sixteen miles long and was operated by horses, for which locomotives were substituted in 1837. The second railway was opened in 1847, and the third in 1848. In 1850 there were only 66 miles of railway in Canada.

The railway era proper may be said to have begun in 1851 with the inauguration of the Grand Trunk system and several subsidiary lines throughout Ontario and Quebec. At Confederation these had grown to 2,278 miles. The Intercolonial, which joined the Maritimes to Quebec and Ontario, was, as already noted, a part of the Confederation compact. The next and most important step was the building of the Canadian Pacific Railway, completed in 1885, which opened and made the whole of the great West an integral part of the Dominion. The second and third transcontinentals, namely, the Canadian Northern Railway and the Grand Trunk Pacific (with the National Transcontinental) belong to the later era of the twentieth century, and their inception is thus within common memory. With their completion Canada possesses the most extensive railway system of any country of its population, no other in the world exceeding us in mileage per capita. According to the latest returns the total steam railway mileage in operation was 40,352; the investments in Canadian rail-

Above—The First Steam Railway Train in Canada, 1837. *Below*—The Quebec Bridge—a Link in the Canadian Government Railway System

Can. Govt. Motion Picture Bureau

ways was approximately three billions; and the gross earnings were $455,000,000. The number of employees in 1925 was 166,027, and the wages bill $238 millions. The Canadian railways carried 41 million passengers and 110 million tons of freight in 1925; in 1875 the traffic was only 5,190,416 passengers and 5,670,837 tons of freight. Ton mileage of revenue freight was 11 billions in 1907 (first year of record) and 32 billions in 1925. The railways use 30 per cent of all the coal consumed in Canada.

The Intercolonial and P.E.I. Railways were from the first owned and operated by the Dominion Government. In 1915, on the failure of the Grand Trunk Pacific Company to take over the National Transcontinental Railway from Moncton, N.B., to Winnipeg, the Government itself undertook its operation, together with that of the Lake Superior Branch of the G.T.P. In 1917, again, the Government acquired the capital stock of the Canadian Northern Railway Company, and in 1919 was appointed receiver for the Grand Trunk Pacific. Later in 1919, the old Grand Trunk was included in the Government railway system, which in 1922 was consolidated and re-organized under a single national board. This great system now controls 22,872 miles of railway, being the largest single system in North America; it includes the Quebec Bridge, which has a central span of 1,800 feet, the longest in the world. Side by side, is the Canadian Pacific with its 14,650 miles of road, its subsidiary steamship lines on the Atlantic and the Pacific, and its historic record in first joining the great west to the Confederation. Besides its importance to Canada, the Canadian Pacific, running in a northern latitude, forms with its auxiliary steamship services a comparatively short way from Europe to the Far East, and thus ranks as one of the great trade routes of the world.

Canada has elaborate machinery for the Government control of transportation in the Board of Railway Commissioners, first organized in 1904, which took over the functions of the Railway Committee of the Privy Council as a rate-controlling body. The Commission has jurisdiction also in matters relating to the location, construction and general operation of railways. To date it has given formal hearings in over 9,000 cases.

Canals.—Canals, as above stated, were the earliest large transportation works in Canada. The first lock was a small one constructed by the Hudson Bay Company at Sault Ste. Marie and was destroyed by U.S. troops in 1814. The next to be built was at the Lachine Rapids in the St. Lawrence above Montreal in 1825, followed by the Welland Canal in 1829 to overcome the obstacle of Niagara Falls. The Rideau Canal (military in primary purpose), the St. Lawrence System and the Chambly Canal followed. To-day there are six canal systems under the Dominion government, namely, (1) between

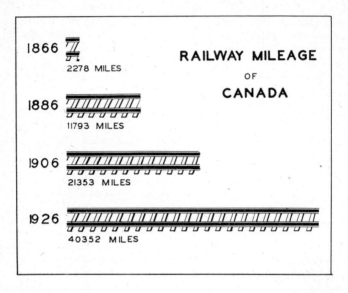

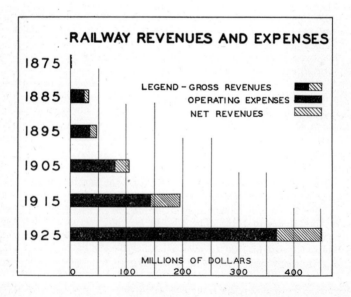

Fort William and Montreal, (2) from Montreal to the International Boundary near lake Champlain, (3) from Montreal to Ottawa, (4) from Ottawa to Kingston, (5) from Trenton to lake Huron and (6) from the Atlantic Ocean to Bras d'Or lakes in Cape Breton. The total length of the waterways comprised in these systems is about 1,594 statute miles. Among projected canals the most important are the

Largest Hydraulic Lift Lock in the World, Peterborough, Ont.
Can. Govt. Motion Picture Bureau

Georgian Bay route and the deepening of the St. Lawrence waterways including the new Welland ship canal. As illustrating growth, freight traffic through the Welland has increased from about 1⅔ million tons in 1872 to 5⅔ millions last year. Canal traffic in 1915 totalled over 14,100,000 tons. Up to date the total capital cost of the Canadian canals is over $189,000,000. It is interesting to note that considerable traffic between the east and west coasts of Canada has in recent years sprung up *via* the Panama Canal.

Electric Railways.—There were horse car systems in Montreal and Toronto as early as 1861, but the first electric street railway, (at St. Catharines, Ont.), dates only from 1887, followed by the Ottawa Electric railway in 1891, and the electrification of the Montreal and Toronto systems in 1892. They are to-day, of course, common to practically all the cities of Canada. Great advances have also been made in the construction and use of suburban or inter-urban electric lines. Altogether there are now some 63 electric railway companies in operation, owning over 2,500 miles of track and about 5,000 cars and with a capitalization of $222 millions. They carry over 725,000,000 fare passengers annually, pay wages of over $24 millions and have a gross revenue of about $50 millions.

Express Companies.—Express service has been defined as "an expedited freight service on passenger trains". The business began in a small way prior to Confederation, and assumed a well developed and permanent form in the 'seventies and 'eighties. There are now 5 systems in operation with a capital somewhat over $9 millions, operating on 45,778 miles of steam and electric railway, boat lines, and stage routes, and with gross receipts of about $25 millions. They issue money orders and travellers' cheques to the amount of between $60 millions and $70 millions annually.

Roads and Highways.—Roads have always been of first importance in Canada. There are to-day about 385,000 miles of highway. Great improvements have taken place under the Good Roads Movement of the past few years, culminating in the Canada Highways Act, which provided a system of grants by the Dominion to the provincial governments in proportion to their own expenditures. Total Dominion aid, under this Act, has been about $18½ millions to date, representing 40 per cent of the expenditure on the approved projects.

Motor Vehicles.—The motor car is, of course, an ultra-modern improvement. Commencing as a toy, and developing as a luxury

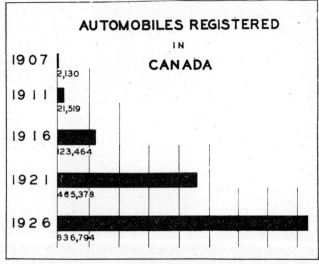

AUTOMOBILES REGISTERED

IN

CANADA

1907 | 2,130

1911 | 21,519

1916 | 123,464

1921 | 465,378

1926 | 836,794

of the rich, it now ranks as a comfort to those in moderate circumstances and a necessity of life to large sections of the population. It is the *raison d'être* of the road improvements just mentioned; it has taken from the railways not only passenger traffic but a large volume of parcel and short-haul freight. The automobile manufacturing industry, since its beginning only twenty years ago, has developed a production of $110,835,380 on a capitalization of $74,678,451, employing about 10,301 persons. Twenty years ago the number of motor vehicles registered in Canada was under 2,000. In 1926 the number was over 800,000, while 205,000 cars and chassis were manufactured in Canada in that year. So omnipresent has the motor car become that it is now customary to state the number in relation to total population. Thus in Nova Scotia in 1925 there was one motor to every 23 of population, in New Brunswick 21, in Quebec 26, in Ontario 9, in Manitoba 13, in Saskatchewan 11, in Alberta 12, and in British Columbia 10. Canada has more motors proportionately (one per 12 people) than any other country except the United States (one per 6).

Air Navigation.—Still more recent as an invention is the aeroplane, which is already of economic importance in the transportation of passengers and supplies to new and remote mining areas, etc. The total mileage of aircraft increased from 185,000 in 1922 to 393,000 in 1926.

Shipping.—The tonnage of sea-going vessels entered and cleared at Canadian ports since Confederation showed an almost continuous increase up to 1914; again since the Armistice there has been a steady increase. The tonnage of coasting vessels has also grown, increasing from 10 million tons in 1876 (the first data compiled) to 83 million tons in 1926, as compared with an increase in sea-going and inland international tonnages from 13 millions in 1868 to 75 millions in 1926.

The vessels on the Canadian shipping registry in 1874 numbered 6,930, with a total tonnage of 1,158,363. They increased in number and tonnage up to 1879, then slowly declined to 1902, when they numbered 6,836 with 652,613 tons. From then on there has been a fairly steady increase in the tonnage, although the number of vessels reached its maximum in 1919 with 8,573, and decreased to 7,913 in 1925, representing 1,283,033 tons.

In the 70's shipbuilding was an important industry in Canada, especially in the Maritime Provinces, when the vessels built were mostly wooden sailing vessels. The invention of the iron steamboat greatly affected the industry in Canada, and there was a more or less steady decline in the numbers of vessels built and registered each year from 1885 to 1914. The war stimulated shipbuilding and there was a temporary activity assisted by the marine programme of the Dominion Government. During the first ten years after Confederation the tonnage of vessels built in Canada aggregated 1,292,000 tons. During the following 7 years 570,000 tons were built, but after 1884 the industry declined rapidly, adding only 369,000 tons for the ten years 1885-1894 and only 222,000 tons for the following decade.

Telegraphs.—Canada's first telegraph line was erected in 1846-7 between Toronto, Hamilton, St. Catharines and Niagara. In 1847 also the Montreal Telegraph Company was organized and a line built to Montreal and Toronto. Other lines rapidly followed, to be brought eventually under the single control of the Great Northwestern Telegraph Company, which remained alone in the field until the building of the Canadian Pacific Railway and the Canadian Government telegraph lines. To-day there are 284,000 miles of telegraph wire in Canada. They handle over 15,000,000 messages, from which the revenue is over $11 millions. In addition, six trans-oceanic cables have a terminus in Canada, five on the Atlantic and one on the Pacific, and handle nearly 6,000,000 cablegrams annually. There is also the Marconi Wireless Telegraph Company and some 34 Government-owned and 74 privately-owned radio telegraph stations, on the east and west sea-coasts and on the Great Lakes. The number of wireless messages handled is now nearly 400,000. Radio telephony has also been established, the total number of radio stations, including private receiving stations, increasing from 33,456 in 1924 to 135,485 in 1926.

Telephones.—The telephone was invented in Canada, and the first talk over any distance was conducted by Alexander Graham Bell and

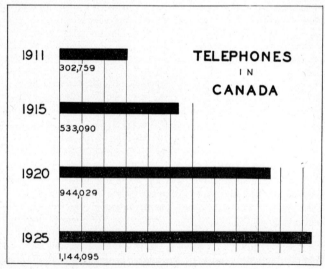

pended but gold payment was resumed as from July 1, 1926. Figures
showing the extension of the Dominion note issue are as follows:—

Year	Dominion Note circulation (averages for the year)
	$
1870*	7,294,103
1880*	13,403,958
1890	15,501,360
1900	26,550,465
1910	89,628,569
1915	159,080,607
1920	305,806,288
1925	212,681,059
1926	190,004,824

*Circulation on June 30.

Bank Notes.—As already stated, Canadians early became accus-
tomed to the free circulation of paper money, and practically all
Canadian banks at their beginning have made the issue of bank notes
their chief means of earning profit. In their early history the holder
of bank notes often lost money when the bank failed, but for the last
forty years no note holder of a failed bank has lost a dollar, as the note
holder has been made the prior creditor in the case of the failure of a
bank. The circulation of bank notes has proceeded on somewhat
parallel lines with that of Dominion notes, as is shown by the figures
below.

Year	Bank Note circulation (averages for the year)
	$
1867*	9,346,086
1870	15,149,031
1880	22,529,623
1890	32,834,511
1900	46,574,780
1910	82,120,303
1915	105,137,092
1920	228,800,379
1925	165,235,168
1926	168,885,995

*Average for six months.

Banking.—About the commencement of the 19th century the
growth of Canadian business was being hampered by the unsatis-
factory and chaotic currency situation. The need for a stable paper
currency was temporarily met by the army bills referred to above,

and after these were redeemed in gold at the end of the war of 1812 the Bank of Montreal commenced business as a bank of note issue in 1817, the Bank of Quebec, the Bank of Canada at Montreal and the Bank of Upper Canada at Kingston in 1818, the Bank of New Brunswick in 1820, and a second Bank of Upper Canada at York in 1821, while the Halifax Banking Company (private) commenced business in 1825 and the Bank of Nova Scotia in 1832. All these banks in the beginning

The Bank of Montreal and the Royal Trust Co., Montreal

N.R.I. Service

made their chief profit out of their note issue. Later banks included the Bank of British North America, which commenced business in Canada in 1836, while Molsons Bank was established in 1853, the Bank of Toronto in 1855, the Banque Nationale in 1860, the Bank Jacques Cartier (later the Banque Provinciale du Canada) in 1862, the Union Bank in 1866, the Canadian Bank of Commerce in 1867, the Merchants Bank of Halifax (now the Royal Bank) in 1869, the Dominion Bank in 1871, the Bank of Hamilton in 1872, the Banque d'Hochelaga in 1873, the Bank of Ottawa in 1874, the Imperial Bank in 1875, and the Standard Bank in 1876.

The increasing service given by the banks to the business community may be measured by the increase in the number of branches. In 1868 there were only 123 branch banks in Canada. In 1902 the number had grown to 747, in 1905 to 1,145, in 1916 to 3,198, and in 1926 to 3,770.

In recent years the banks of Canada have extended their business outside of the country itself and at the close of 1926 had among them 195 branches in foreign countries, mainly in Newfoundland, the British and foreign West Indies, Central and South America, and also in the great centres of international finance, London, Paris and New York.

Through the operation of the clearing houses, a record of inter-bank transactions has been maintained since the opening of the first clearing-house in 1889, and form a valuable indication of the trend of business. Thus the clearings at Montreal, the commercial metropolis of Canada, were $454 millions in 1889, reached $1,098 millions in 1902, $2,088 millions in 1910, $3,722 millions in 1916, $6,254 millions in 1919, and $7,109 millions in 1920 at the height of the inflation period. This, however, does not tell the whole story, since every amalgamation of banks lessens in so far the volume of clearings. Accordingly, a record of cheques debited to accounts at all branches at clearing house centres was instituted in 1924; between that date and 1926 Montreal bank debits increased from $7,502 millions to $9,133 millions, and the grand total of bank debits for Canada from $27,157 millions to $30,358 millions—an increase of nearly 12 per cent in two years.

The expansion of the assets of Canadian banks since 1867 is shown graphically in the diagram on the opposite page. The 1920 and 1921 figures, in particular, are swollen by the post-war inflation of the currency. Certainly, the bank assets of 1926, equated with current prices, represent a greater purchasing power than in any previous year.

Insurance

Life Insurance.—The life insurance business was introduced into Canada by companies from the British Isles and the United States and was taken up almost as early along the same general lines by a native company. Among the first companies to transact life insurance business in Canada may be mentioned:—Scottish Amicable (1846), Standard (1847), Canada Life (1847), Ætna (1850), Liverpool and London and Globe (1851), and Royal (1851). No fewer than 14 companies began business in the early 70's, including four native companies, namely:—Sun (incorporated 1865, began business 1871), Mutual of Canada (Ontario Mutual, 1870), Confederation (1871) and London (1874). By 1875 there were at least 26 companies and possibly several more, competing for the available business in Canada, as against 45 companies licensed by the Dominion and a few provincial companies in 1924.

The development of life insurance in Canada, as in other English-speaking countries at least, has been marked by an increased service to the individual policy-holder. The benefits which may now be obtained under a life insurance policy are calculated to meet the needs

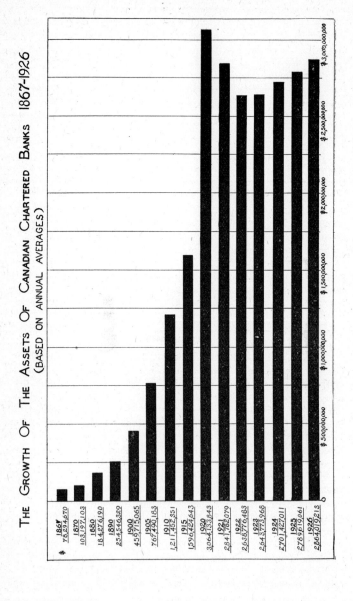

THE GROWTH OF THE ASSETS OF CANADIAN CHARTERED BANKS 1867-1926
(BASED ON ANNUAL AVERAGES)

Year	Amount
1867	78,894,670
1870	103,197,103
1880	184,276,190
1890	254,546,329
1900	459,715,065
1905	767,490,183
1910	1,211,452,351
1915	1,590,424,643
1920	3,064,133,843
1921	2,841,782,079
1922	2,638,776,483
1923	2,643,773,968
1924	2,701,427,011
1925	2,789,619,061
1926	2,864,019,213

of the policy holder and of his dependants, whether in event of old age or in event of death or of permanent disability. Policies may be obtained under which, if the policy holder becomes unable to follow any occupation by reason of ill-health or accident, not only do premiums cease, but in addition he receives an income under the policy without any reduction in the benefits formerly accruing to the beneficiary at the death of the insured. Within the last few years there has been introduced what is known as "group insurance", a plan whereby a group of persons, usually employees, are insured by their employer, for a uniform amount or a varying amount determined by a formula, under one policy, generally on the term plan, the employer paying the premium or a substantial part thereof, each employee having the right to obtain an individual policy at ordinary normal rates, without medical examination, on termination of employment.

As a result of the adaptation of life insurance policies to the needs of the public, and of the growing wealth of the community, the growth in the amount of life insurance in force has been phenomenal. In 1869 the total life insurance in force in Dominion companies was only $35,680,000 as compared with $4,609,900,000 at the end of 1926. The increase in the life insurance in force in Canada during the single year 1926 was greater than the total amount in force in Canada in 1900.

This remarkable growth is graphically shown in the diagram on the following page.

Fire Insurance.—Fire insurance in Canada began with the establishment by British fire insurance companies of agencies, usually situated in the sea ports and operated by local merchants. The oldest existing agency of a British company is that of the Phœnix Fire Office of London, now the Phœnix Assurance Co. Ltd., which commenced business in Montreal in 1804.

The Halifax Fire Insurance Co. is the first purely Canadian company of which any record is obtainable. Founded in 1809 as the Nova Scotia Fire Association, it was chartered in 1819 and operated in the province of Nova Scotia until 1919, when it was granted a Dominion license. Among the other pioneer fire insurance companies still in operation, mention may be made of the following:—the Quebec Fire Assurance Co., which commenced business in 1818 and was largely confined in ownership and operations to Quebec province; the British America Assurance Co., incorporated in 1833, the oldest company in Ontario; the Western Assurance Co., organized in 1851 and, after a rapid and steady growth, one of the largest companies of its kind on the continent; two American companies, the Ætna Insurance Co., of Hartford, Conn., and the Hartford Fire Insurance Co., which commenced business in Canada in 1821 and 1836 respectively.

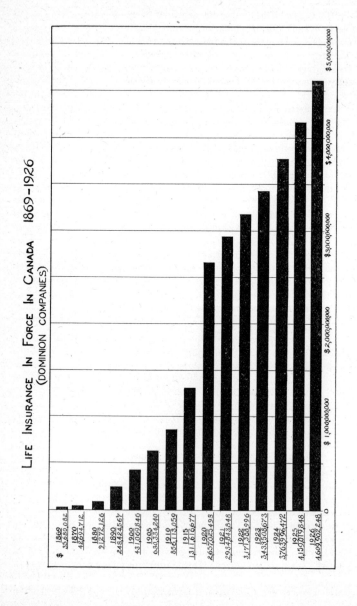

LIFE INSURANCE IN FORCE IN CANADA 1869–1926
(DOMINION COMPANIES)

The report of the Superintendent of Insurance for the year ended Dec. 31, 1925, shows that at that date there were 188 fire insurance companies doing business in Canada under Dominion licenses, of which 43 were Canadian, 59 were British and 86 were foreign companies, whereas in 1875, the first year for which authentic records were collected by the Insurance Department, 27 companies operated in Canada, 11 Canadian, 13 British and 3 American. The proportionate increase in the number of British and foreign companies from 59 to 77 p.c. of the total number is a very marked point of difference between the fire and life insurance businesses in Canada, the latter being carried on very largely by Canadian companies.

The enormous increase since 1869 (the earliest year for which we have statistics) in the fire insurance in force, is no doubt partly due to the growth of the practice of insurance, but it is also important as an indication of the growth of the value of insurable property in the country, and thus throws light upon the expansion of the national wealth of Canada. At the end of 1925, besides the $7,597 millions of fire insurance in force in companies with Dominion licenses, there were also $1,215 millions in force in companies with provincial licenses, and $566 millions in force with companies, associations, or underwriters not licensed to transact business in Canada, or a grand total of $9,378 millions of fire insurance in force in the Dominion.

The trend of the growth of fire insurance in force in companies licensed by the Dominion Government is indicated by the following figures.

Year	Fire insurance in force at end of year
	$
1866	188,359,809
1880	411,563,271
1890	720,679,621
1900	992,332,360
1910	2,034,276,740
1920	5,969,872,278
1925	7,597,224,627
1926*	8,045,437,096

*Preliminary figure.

Miscellaneous Insurance.—Since 1875 the growth of insurance business other than fire and life has been a steady one. The report of the Superintendent of Insurance for the calendar year 1880 shows that the number of companies duly licensed for the transaction of accident, guarantee, plate glass and steam boiler insurance—the only four classes of miscellaneous insurance then transacted—was 5, 3, 1 and 1 respectively. The same report for the year 1924 shows that miscellaneous insurance now includes in Canada, accident, sickness, automobile, burglary, explosion, forgery, guarantee, hail, inland transportation, employers' liability, aviation, plate glass, sprinkler-leakage, steam boiler, title, tornado and live stock insurance, etc. Whereas in 1880, 10 companies transacted business of this kind, such insurance was sold in 1925 by 169 companies, of which 35 were Canadian and 134 British and foreign.

The most important class of miscellaneous insurance, according to the amount of premiums received, is automobile insurance, which has greatly increased in recent years. As recently as 1910, the premium income of companies doing an automobile insurance business was only $80,446; in 1915 it was $573,604 and in 1925 $6,950,856. Hail insurance companies ranked second, with a premium income in 1925 of $5,397,594.

Loan and Trust Companies

Loan Companies.—Business such as that now transacted by loan companies was first carried on by an incorporated Canadian company in 1844, when the Lambton Loan and Investment Co. was established. In order to legalize and encourage such operations, an Act to this end was passed by the Legislature of Canada in 1846, followed in 1847 and 1849 by similar Acts in New Brunswick and Nova Scotia respectively. These early companies were termed building societies; their activities comprised mainly the lending of money on security of real estate and also the lending of money to members without their being liable to the contingency of losses or profits in the business of the society. In addition to these operations, such companies were authorized, by an Act of 1859, to "borrow money to a limited extent." Later, by the Building Societies Act of 1874, authority was given to receive money on deposit and to issue debentures subject to certain restrictions as to amounts of deposits.

The principal function of loan companies is the lending of funds on first mortgage security, the money thus made available for development purposes being secured mainly by the sale of debentures to the investing public and by savings department deposits. Of the loan companies operating under provincial charters, the majority conduct loan, savings and mortgage business, generally in the more prosperous farming communities.

The number of loan and savings societies in operation and making returns to the Government at Confederation was 19, with an aggregate paid-up capital of $2,110,403 and deposits of $577,299. Rapid increases in the number of companies and total volume of business resulted from subsequent legislation until in 1899, 102 companies made returns, showing capital stock paid up of $47,337,544, reserve funds of $9,923,728 and deposits of \$19,466,676; total liabilities had increased from \$3,233,985 to \$148,143,496 between 1867 and 1899. After slight decreases in the number of loan companies in operation shortly after the turn of the century, further increases were again recorded until in 1925 a total of 124 companies were in existence in Canada, with total liabilities of \$118,139,081 to the public and \$78,925,549 to the shareholders—or a grand total of \$197,064,630.

Trust Companies.—Trust companies act as executors, trustees and administrators under wills or by appointment, as trustees under marriage or other settlements, as agents or attorneys in the management of the estates of the living, as guardians of minor or incapable persons, as financial agents for municipalities and companies and, where so appointed, as authorized trustees in bankruptcy. Some companies receive deposits but the lending of actual trust funds is restricted by law.

Trust companies are principally provincial institutions, since their original main functions are connected with probate, which lies within the sole jurisdiction of the provinces. The aggregate total assets of the trust companies of Canada, whether operating under Dominion or under provincial licenses, show an increase from \$805 millions in 1922 (the earliest year for which this figure is available), to \$934 millions in 1925. Of this enormous amount, \$830 millions was in estates, trusts and agency funds.

CHAPTER XVII.—THE LABOUR MOVEMENT

The trade union movement as we know it to-day has developed almost wholly since Confederation. There were sporadic unions in existence as far back as the 'thirties, and certain of these, notably in Toronto and Montreal, attained to considerable importance in the 'forties and 'fifties. But until the establishment of the factory system and the gathering of workers in industrial centres, trade unionism does not ordinarily arise, especially in a country of simple wants and abundant unclaimed natural resources. Moreover, it was not until 1872 that liberty of association, the corner-stone of trade unionism, was won in Canada (after a famous trial in Toronto and following the repeal of the Combination laws in England in the previous year). This and the current industrial activity gave a spur to organization and in 1873 the first step was taken towards organizing a general association or congress of the Canadian labour bodies. "The Canadian Labour Union" formed in that year lapsed in the industrial depression of 1875, and though organization efforts on a local basis persisted and some notable gains were made in the years immediately following, no permanent central association again arose until 1883, when the "Trades and Labour Congress of Canada", destined to become the most powerful central representative of organized labour in Canada, was formed. This body has never since gone out of existence, holding annual sessions that have constituted the chief vehicle for the expression of labour opinion in Canada. Meanwhile, several other central bodies have arisen and given additional voice to the views of labour.

The great majority of the local trade unions of Canada occupy a unique position by reason of the fact that they are branches of central craft organizations which embrace the whole continent and have their headquarters in the United States. For that reason they are termed "international" unions. As the American Federation of Labour is the principal federal representative for purposes of legislative discussion of these central craft associations in the United States, so in Canada the Trades and Labour Congress represents the unions affiliated with the "internationals". There are, however, certain large international unions, notably in railroad employment, which do not affiliate with the Federation or the Congress. Thus Canada, while deriving its labour organization machinery very largely from the continental system, maintains its legislative independence. The Trades and Labour Congress, it may be added, is a member of the International Federation of Trade Unions, commonly known as the "Amsterdam International", to which only one central body from each country is admitted.

The international unions, however, though the preponderant body, by no means make up the entirety of the Canadian labour movement. In addition there have always been a number of purely national unions, some of which, such as the Provincial Workmen's Association

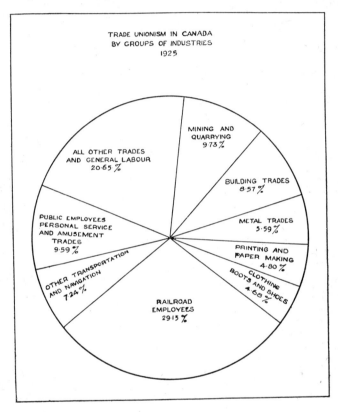

of Nova Scotia and the Canadian Federation of Labour, have long and interesting histories. At the present time the leading exponents of national Unionism are the "National and Catholic" unions of Quebec, numbering 103 branches and having a total membership of over 25,000, and the "All-Canadian Congress of Labour" which in turn embraces the Canadian Brotherhood of Railroad Employees (14,500 members), the One Big Union (18,665 members), the Electrical Communication Workers (1,400 members), and some others. There are also some 38 independent Canadian labour units.

Reviewing labour organization in Canada as a whole, there were in 1926 some 2,515 local trade unions, having a combined membership of 274,604. In 1911, the earliest year for which there are records there were but 1,722 local unions, having a membership of 133,132. The "peak" year was 1919, when there were 378,047 organized trade unionists in Canada, in 2,847 local branches.

As stated above, most of these are branches of the international craft unions, the number of such at present being 2,011, having a membership of 179,276, representing some 89 associations. The stronger of these latter bodies are:—

Name of organization	Number of Canadian Local Units	Reported membership of Canadian Units
United Mine Workers of America	39	14,820
Brotherhood of Railroad Trainmen	96	14,250
Brotherhood of Railway Carmen	113	12,356
International Association of Machinists	84	8,046
American Federation of Musicians	42	8,000
Amalgamated Association of Street and Electric Railway Employees	26	7,500
Brotherhood of Railroad Telegraphers	13	7,438
United Brotherhood of Carpenters and Joiners	84	7,341
Brotherhood of Locomotive Firemen and Enginemen	104	7,171
Brotherhood of Locomotive Engineers	103	6,503
Brotherhood of Maintenance-of-Way Employees	185	5,984

The Trades and Labour Councils are important bodies in the Canadian scheme of labour organization. Altogether there are over 40 of these in Canada, each being the local medium for the expression of views on public questions. There are also some 50 "District Councils" of labour, and an equal number of labour "Federations."

Naturally, the larger cities are the chief homes of trade unionism, thirty cities of Canada having twenty or more local unions, Montreal ranking first with 194, Toronto second with 139, Winnipeg third with 96, Vancouver fourth with 95, and Ottawa and Calgary fifth and sixth with 66 and 64 respectively.

The percentage of organized workers to total population in Canada is lower than in most of the countries of Europe or in Australia or New Zealand. It is, however, not radically different from that of the United States, with which comparison is naturally made (2·9 p.c. compared with 3.4 p.c.). This low percentage doubtless reflects the preponderance of agriculture in our industrial structure, as well as the general stage of economic development that has been reached in the country, including such factors as the proximity of free land, the relatively high rate of immigration, etc., all of which have a strong reaction on the tendency to organize. The distribution of the trade unionists of Canada among the industries of the country is shown by percentages in the diagram on page 123.

Accompanying the steady progress of trade unionism have been many developments of the first importance to Canadian labour. In 1900 occurred the establishment of the Dominion Department of Labour, whose duties are to aid in the prevention and settlement of labour disputes, to collect and disseminate information relative to labour conditions, to administer the government's fair wages policy and in general to investigate problems involving the interests of workers. Under the first mentioned of these functions, the Industrial Disputes Investigation Act, originated in 1907 for the settlement of trade disputes, has attracted favourable comment throughout the world; over 650 threatened disputes have been referred under it to date, and in all but some 40 cases an open break has been averted. A monthly "Labour Gazette" has, since 1900, provided a comprehensive survey of labour conditions in Canada and is supplemented by various special publications. The Department also has more recently established the "Employment Service of Canada", which copes with the unemployment problem, and it administers the Technical Education Act, the Government Annuities Act and the Combines Investigation Acts—the latter being a measure aimed at combinations in restraint of trade. In addition, the department acts generally as the representative in Canada of the International Labour Office of the League of Nations, Canada as one of the eight states of "chief industrial importance" having a place on the Governing Body of that Office. In several of the provinces likewise, namely, in Quebec, Ontario, Manitoba, Saskatchewan, Alberta and British Columbia, Departments or bureaus of labour have been set up. Under these are administered an increasing body of legislation of various kinds ("civil rights" pertaining to the provinces under the B.N.A. Act) in the form of factories, shops and mines acts, workmen's compensation acts (most of the provinces having special boards for the administration of the latter legislation), laws for the protection of women and children in industry, mechanics' lien acts and other legislation for the safeguarding of wages, etc., etc. The growth of this body of legislation is one of the most outstanding features of social progress in the present century.

The final weapon of organized labour is the strike. Records of strikes go back to the beginning of the century, in which year 104 strikes were in existence, involving 28,086 employees and a time loss of 632,302 working days. In 1903 and again in 1911-1912-1913 the losses were heavy. The highest loss, however, occurred in 1919 when there were 298 strikes involving 138,988 employees with a time loss of

3,942,189 working days. In 1926 there were 77 strikes, involving about 24,000 working people and a time loss of 296,811 days. Generally speaking, the time loss through strikes has been proportionately less in Canada than in other industrial countries.

Labour has latterly come to play a noteworthy part in Canadian politics. The first election of a Labour member to a provincial legislature occurred in 1873. From time to time this was repeated in other provinces and in the Dominion Parliament. For many years, however, no definite political policy was adopted by labour. It was not until 1917 that the present "Canadian Labour Party" had its origin in a suggestion of the Trades and Labour Congress; it has now completed the organization of provincial sections in Nova Scotia, Quebec, Ontario, Manitoba, Saskatchewan, Alberta and British Columbia. There is also an Independent Labour party in Ontario and Manitoba. In the federal election held in October, 1925, twenty straight Labour candidates appeared, one being termed a Farmer-Labour candidate and one an Independent Labour candidate. Three were elected. Several of the Provincial Legislatures have labour members.

Large sums on account of benefits are expended by labour organizations. For both Canada and the United States these in 1926 amounted to the high total of over $22 millions. Canada's share in this is unknown, but, apart from amounts received from headquarters of international organizations, expenditures in Canada on benefits for 1926 amounted to $316,922, the chief items being sick and accident benefits, death benefits and strike benefits.

Side by side with labour organization has been a strong movement in Canada towards the formation of employers' associations. These involve a wide variety of business enterprises, and aggregate statements are somewhat meaningless. Altogether, however, the Department of Labour has collected records in 1926 of 1,318 associations of employers, reporting a membership of 1,238,812. These figures, it should be added, include co-operative associations (producers) to the number of 704, with a membership of 265,423, professional associations (legal, medical, dental, etc.) to the number of 165, with a membership of 86,148, as well as agricultural, dairying and live stock breeders' associations of various kinds whose membership runs over 825,000.

CHAPTER XVIII.—EDUCATION IN CANADA

The first census to be taken after Confederation (1871) showed 20 per cent of the people over the age of 20 years as "illiterate", in the sense of being unable to read or write; 681,891 persons as "going to school"; 5,145 as "inmates" of universities and classical colleges; and 7,756 as at boarding schools for young ladies. The number of universities and colleges was then 75, and that of boarding schools 162. The number mentioned as teachers was 13,400, and as professors, 264. This may be regarded as representing the general status of education and of educational activities at the time of Confederation, when the system was simple in the extreme.

With the above figures may be contrasted the following—though it should be pointed out at once that the chief element of contrast between the two periods lies in the complexity and ramifying character of present-day education. In 1921 the proportion of illiteracy was but 5 per cent in the population over 10 years of age. In all educational institutions there were 2,228,869 pupils and students in 1925; 1,965,852 were in publicly controlled kindergarten, elementary and high schools; 72,104 in private schools of the same nature; 4,955 in preparatory courses to universities and colleges (high school pupils today, but probably considered as "college" students in earlier days); 95,684 in technical and night courses in schools mostly under public control; 1,560 in schools for the deaf and blind; over 16,000 in private business colleges; 14,222 in Indian schools; 9,899 in classical colleges; 8,531 in regular courses in other colleges; 22,723 in regular courses in universities; and 10,220 in schools for teacher training. A close estimate shows that the number of pupils in elementary grades was 1,896,954 and in secondary grades 267,797, the remainder being in night and other schools of which the status of the pupils was difficult to determine,

Turning to the teaching end: In 1925 there were over 65,000 teachers in Canada in ordinary and technical schools; 3,864 professors in universities and their preparatory schools; 1,829 in colleges and their preparatory schools; and about 5,000 between private schools, business colleges and Indian schools. While some allowance must be made for duplications, the number in the teaching profession including higher education is therefore not far short of 76,000. The accompanying table gives the present-day facts *re* education in Canada in summary.

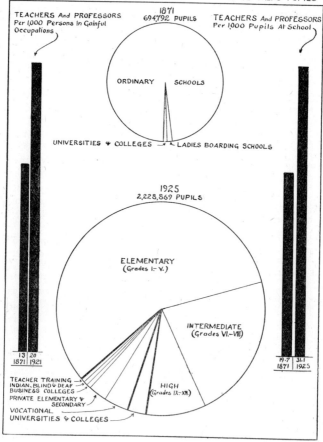

EDUCATION IN CANADA SINCE CONFEDERATION
DEVELOPMENT AND GROWTH:— INSTITUTIONS—TEACHERS—PUPILS

TEACHERS And PROFESSORS
Per 1,000 Persons In Gainful
Occupations

TEACHERS And PROFESSORS
Per 1,000 Pupils At School

1871
694,792 PUPILS

ORDINARY   SCHOOLS

UNIVERSITIES & COLLEGES — — LADIES BOARDING SCHOOLS

1925
2,228,869 PUPILS

ELEMENTARY
(Grades I.- V.)

INTERMEDIATE
(Grades VI.-VIII)

HIGH
(Grades IX.-XII)

TEACHER TRAINING —
INDIAN, BLIND & DEAF —
BUSINESS COLLEGES —
PRIVATE ELEMENTARY &
SECONDARY —
VOCATIONAL —
UNIVERSITIES & COLLEGES —

13 | 20
1871 | 1921

19.7 | 31.1
1871 | 1925

Education in Canada, 1925: Educational Institutions, Pupils, Teachers and Expenditures

Type of institution	Number	Number of pupils	Number of teachers	Expenditure
				$
Ordinary day schools under public control.............	29,589	1,965,832	59,030	⎫
Schools for teacher training..	58	10,220	514	⎪ 116,664,761[1]
Schools for blind and deaf....	11	1,561	300[2]	⎬
Technical and night schools..	351	95,684	5,379	⎭
Private, elementary and secondary schools and business colleges....................	685	88,150	4,658	
Indian schools...............	333	14,222	333[2]	2,000,000[3]
Universities and colleges.....	102	57,949	5,693	14,779,503[4]
Total...............	31,129	2,228,869[5]	75,907	133,443,264[6]

[1] Including $9,043,636 of subsidized independent schools in Quebec. This item is not entered under private schools as it does not represent all private schools.

[2] Approximate.

[3] Approximate. The Dominion Government in 1925 contributed $1,854,609 and the Indians themselves $65,496. The expenditures by churches, etc., are not given.

[4] Including only about $6,000,000 in Government grants. The remainder was paid from investments, fees and other sources.

[5] Less 4,749 duplicates.

[6] This includes debenture payments, building, grounds, etc.

The list of institutions given in this table affords a fair idea of the scope of educational activities carried on at the present. It may be added that the technical and high schools, while not entirely peculiar to the present century—since there were agricultural and technical schools in existence, especially in Quebec, at a very early date—represent an opportunity largely confined to the present generation, if not the present century, by far the greatest growth having taken place since the war. It may further illustrate the increased scope of educational activities to mention that about 280,000 persons in educational institutions are now practically adults, i.e., are either over 16 years of age or are in classes designed for persons who have discontinued attendance at ordinary schools. In addition to the above should be mentioned the new work for the mentally and physically subnormal; medical and nurse inspection of schools; the effective child labour and compulsory attendance laws recently enacted; the consolidation of schools, with conveyance of children to schools, and the creation of municipal school districts, rural graded schools and rural high schools— all designed to secure larger taxation areas and thus support better classes of schools—bringing high school education within the reach of rural children, creating rural centres with community halls (thus increasing social opportunities in rural communities), providing facilities for teaching such subjects as manual training, domestic science, if not vocational or semi-vocational work, etc., etc.

Of the twenty-three universities now in existence, sixteen date from before Confederation; of the 85 colleges, including classical colleges, 24 date from before Confederation. The larger universities are now devoting much attention to scientific research, perhaps the most notable achievement up to the present being the discovery of insulin, a preparation which indefinitely prolongs the lives of diabetics, by Dr. F. G. Banting and Mr. C. H. Best, of the University of Toronto; the former received the Nobel prize in medicine in 1923—an outstanding mark of international appreciation of his achievement.

A Consolidated Rural School

Can. Govt. Motion Picture Bureau

As already said, our progress since Confederation cannot be measured by statistics alone. For example, in measuring the results of education by the illiteracy figures of the census, the enormous task that Canada has had to face in the illiteracy created by the inrush of foreign-born—a task which is not reflected in the figures of illiteracy and attendance at educational institutions in 1867—must be considered. To say that the reduction of illiteracy between 1871 and 1921 was from 20 per cent to 5 per cent is but a partial measurement of Canadian achievement, since the population was largely homogeneous in 1871 whereas it is to-day far otherwise. The problem of illiteracy has been created as well as largely solved since Confederation.

A feature also to be emphasized is the growth of secondary education. At Confederation it included some elementary work, also high school and what is now university work; in reality it pertained to university education, the high school in its present sense being in consequence unknown. At a later date it came to include the academic and professional training of teachers, so that the secondary school was either a preparatory school for universities or a vocational school for teachers. The high school of to-day, on the other hand, is a continuation of the elementary school—a means of extending general education without reference to vocation. How far the high school has travelled may be seen from the fact that in 1925 high school grades enrolled over 200,000 pupils, while only about 10,000 were in normal schools and about 32,000 were in regular courses at universities and colleges. Thus, it is likely that about 160,000, or 80 per cent of these, looked forward neither to university work or to the teaching profession, but were attending high school merely to extend their general education. High school work to-day can be taken in almost any rural school and if the pupil has thus qualified to write departmental examinations he receives a certificate of his academic training which is usually taken at its face value by business men and by the public at large.

The proportions entering high school have increased enormously since the beginning of the present century. Until that date only the exceptional pupil completed elementary work and entered upon high school work. To-day about 35 per cent of those who go to school at all do some high school work—either ordinary, technical or agricultural high school. Further, owing to regular attendance and better methods of teaching, the pupil is ready for continuation work a year or two earlier than at the beginning of the century, so that to meet the requirements of compulsory attendance and child labour laws he must stay at school and do continuation work; further, practically all the pupils who go to school at all and are mentally capable of completing elementary work are to-day reaching a stage of education at which they are ready to do continuation work. The high schools are crowded. The technical day school pupil who was almost non-existent a few years ago is now to the ordinary high school pupil in the proportion of one to seven, but at the present rate of increase of those ready for continuation work the enrolment in the technical schools may eventually exceed that of the high schools. Continuation work has increased at an unparalleled rate but the demand for it has increased at a much greater rate.

A still more important feature, but one which cannot be briefly described, is the raising of the status of the teacher. In earlier times the trained teacher was the exception. To-day, with about 60,000 ordinary teaching positions, there are over 10,000 in schools for teacher training. It is becoming not unusual to find university graduates teaching in the elementary schools. Further, the universities now give short courses for teachers during the summer, elementary teachers spending a part of their vacation thereat to improve their standing, while a regular system of conventions enables them to exchange ideas and solve their various problems. Teaching is no longer a stepping stone to something else, but is in itself a learned profession.

The above considerations must be borne in mind when discussing expenditures on education. In 1924-25, including all institutions, this expenditure was about $133,000,000, but this included in some cases endowments of universities and colleges, and in most cases debenture payments for debts incurred on building before and during the war. These and other facts, including the fact that the dollar of 1925 has only the purchasing power of 80 cents in 1867, render comparison of the expenditure on education in 1925 with that of an early date to a large extent profitless, except as demonstrating what the people of Canada are willing to pay for education.

APPENDIX I

Chronology of Confederated Canada

1864. Conferences on Confederation of British North America: Sept. 1, at Charlottetown; Oct. 10-29, at Quebec.
1865. Feb. 3, The Canadian Legislature resolves on an address to the Queen praying for union of the provinces of British North America. Oct. 20, Proclamation fixing the seat of government at Ottawa.
1866. March 17, Termination of the Reciprocity Treaty by the United States. May 31, Raid of Fenians from the United States into Canada; they are defeated at Ridgeway (June 2) and retreat across the border (June 3).
1867. March 29, Royal assent given to the British North America Act. July 1, the Act comes into force; Union of the provinces of Canada, Nova Scotia and New Brunswick as the Dominion of Canada; Upper and Lower Canada made separate provinces as Ontario and Quebec; Viscount Monck first Governor-General, Sir John A. Macdonald premier. Nov. 6, Meeting of the first Dominion Parliament.
1868. July 31, The Rupert's Land Act authorizes the acquisition by the Dominion of the Northwest Territories.
1869. Feb. 2, Lord Lisgar takes office as Governor-General. June 22, Act providing for the government of the Northwest Territories. Outbreak of the Red River Rebellion under Riel.
1870. May 12, Act to establish the province of Manitoba. July 15, Northwest Territories transferred to the Dominion and Manitoba admitted into Confederation.
1871. April 2, First Dominion Census. April 14, Act establishing uniform currency in the Dominion. May 8, Treaty of Washington, dealing with questions outstanding between the United Kingdom and United States. July 20, British Columbia enters Confederation.
1872. June 25, The Earl of Dufferin takes office as Governor-General.
1873. March 5, Opening of the second Dominion Parliament. July 1, Prince Edward Island enters Confederation. Nov. 7, Alexander Mackenzie premier.
1874. March 26, Opening of the third Dominion Parliament.
1875. April 8, The Northwest Territories Act establishes a Lieutenant-Governor and Council of the Northwest Territories.
1876. June 5, First sitting of the Supreme Court of Canada. July 3, Opening of the Intercolonial Railway from Quebec to Halifax.
1877. June 20, Great fire at St. John, N.B.
1878. July 1, Canada joins the International Postal Union. Oct. 17, Sir J. A. Macdonald, premier. Nov. 25, The Marquis of Lorne takes office as Governor-General.
1879. Feb. 13, Opening of the fourth Dominion Parliament. May 15, Adoption of a protective tariff ("The National Policy").
1880. May 11, Sir A. T. Galt appointed first Canadian High Commissioner in London. Sept. 1, All British possessions in North America and adjacent islands, except Newfoundland and its dependencies, annexed to Canada by Imperial Order in Council of July 31. Oct. 21, Signing of the contract for the construction of the Canadian Pacific railway.
1881. April 4, Second Dominion census. May 2, First sod turned of the Canadian Pacific railway.
1882. May 8, Provisional Districts of Assiniboia, Saskatchewan, Athabaska and Alberta formed.
1883. Feb. 1, Opening of the fifth Dominion Parliament. Oct. 23, The Marquis of Lansdowne takes office as Governor-General.

1885. March 26, Outbreak of Riel's second rebellion in the Northwest. May 12, Taking of Batoche. May 16, Surrender of Riel.
1886. June 28, First through train on the Canadian Pacific railway from Montreal to Vancouver.
1887. April 13, Opening of the sixth Dominion Parliament.
1888. June 11, Lord Stanley of Preston takes office as Governor-General.
1891. April 5, Third Dominion census. April 29, Opening of the seventh Dominion Parliament. June 6, Death of Sir J. A. Macdonald. June 15, Sir John Abbott, premier.
1892. Feb. 29, Washington Treaty, providing for arbitration of the Behring Sea Seal Fisheries question. Nov. 25, Sir John Thompson, premier.
1893. Sept. 18, The Earl of Aberdeen takes office as Governor-General.
1894. June 28, Colonial Conference at Ottawa. Dec. 12, Death of Sir John Thompson at Windsor Castle. Dec. 21, (Sir) Mackenzie Bowell, premier.
1895. Sept. 10, Opening of new Sault Ste. Marie canal. Oct. 2, Proclamation naming the Ungava, Franklin, Mackenzie and Yukon districts of Northwest Territories.
1896. April 24, Sir Donald Smith (Lord Strathcona), High Commissioner in London. April 27, Sir Charles Tupper, premier. July 11, (Sir) Wilfrid Laurier, premier. Aug. 19, Opening of the eighth Dominion Parliament.
1897. July, Third Colonial Conference in London.
1898. June 13, The Yukon district established as a separate territory. Aug. 1, The British Preferential Tariff of Canada goes into force. Nov. 12, The Earl of Minto takes office as Governor-General. Dec. 25, British Imperial Penny (2 cent) Postage introduced.
1899. Oct. 11, Beginning of the South African war. Oct. 29, First Canadian contingent leaves Quebec for South Africa.
1900. Feb. 27, Battle of Paardeberg.
1901. Jan. 22, Death of Queen Victoria and accession of King Edward VII. Feb. 6, Opening of the ninth Dominion Parliament. April 1, Fourth Dominion census.
1902. June 30, Meeting of fourth Colonial Conference in London.
1903. Jan. 24, Signing of the Alaska Boundary Convention.
1904. April 19, Great fire in Toronto. Dec. 10, The Earl Grey takes office as Governor-General.
1905. Jan. 11, Opening of the tenth Dominion Parliament. Sept. 1, Creation of the provinces of Alberta and Saskatchewan.
1906. University of Alberta founded.
1907. April 15-May 14, Fifth Colonial Conference in London. New customs tariff, including introduction of intermediate tariff. Sept. 19, New Commercial convention with France signed at Paris. University of Saskatchewan founded.
1908. Jan. 2, Establishment of Ottawa branch of Royal Mint. July 20-31, Quebec tercentenary celebrations: visit to Quebec of the Prince of Wales. University of British Columbia founded.
1909. Jan. 20, Opening of 11th Dominion Parliament. July 28, Conference on Imperial Defence in London.
1910. May 4, Passing of Naval Service Bill. May 6, Death of King Edward VII and accession of King George V. New trade agreement made with Germany, Belgium, Holland and Italy.
1911. May 23-June 20, Imperial Conference in London. June 1, Fifth Dominion census. Sept. 21, General election. Oct. 10 (Sir) R. L. Borden, premier. Oct. 11, Inauguration at Kitchener of Ontario hydro-electric power transmission system. Oct. 13, His Royal Highness the Duke of Connaught takes office as Governor-General. Nov. 15, Opening of 12th Dominion Parliament.
1912. May 15, Extension of the boundaries of Quebec, Ontario and Manitoba.
1913. June 2, Trade agreement with West Indies came into force.
1914. Aug. 4, War with Germany; Aug. 12, with Austria-Hungary; Nov. 5, with Turkey. Aug. 18-22, Special war session of Canadian Parliament. Oct. 16, First Canadian contingent of over 33,000 troops lands at Plymouth, Eng.

1915. Feb., First Canadian contingent lands in France and proceeds to Flanders. April 22, Second battle of Ypres. April 24, Battle of St. Julien. May 20-26, Battle of Festubert. June 15, Battle of Givenchy; gallantry of Canadian troops highly eulogized by F.-M. Sir John French.

1916. Jan. 12, Order in Council authorizing increase in number of Canadian troops to 500,000. Feb. 3, Destruction of Houses of Parliament at Ottawa by fire. April 3-20, Battle of St. Eloi. June 1, Census of Prairie Provinces. June 1-3, Battle of Sanctuary Wood. Nov. 11, The Duke of Devonshire takes office as Governor-General.

1917. Feb. 12-May 15, Imperial Conference. Mar. 21-April 27, Imperial War Conference. April 5, United States declares war against Germany. April 9, Capture of Vimy Ridge. Aug. 15, Battle of Loos, capture of Hill 70. Oct. 26-Nov. 10, Battle of Passchendaele. Dec. 6, Disastrous explosion at Halifax, N.S. Dec. 17, General election and Union Government sustained.

1918. Mar. 18, Opening of first session of 13th Parliament. Mar.-April, Second battle of the Somme. July 18, Allies assume successful offensive on west front. Aug. 12, Battle of Amiens. Aug. 26-28, Capture of Monchy le Preux. Sept. 2-4, Breaking of Drocourt-Quéant line. Sept. 16, Austrian peace note. Sept. 27-29, Capture of Bourlon Wood. Sept. 30, Bulgaria surrenders and signs armistice. Oct. 1-9, Capture of Cambrai. Oct. 6, First German peace note. Oct. 20, Capture of Denain. Oct. 25-Nov. 2, Capture of Valenciennes. Oct. 31, Turkey surrenders and signs armistice. Nov. 4, Austria-Hungary surrenders and signs armistice. Nov. 10, Flight of German Emperor into Holland. Capture of Mons. Nov. 11, Germany surrenders and signs armistice.

1919. Feb. 17, Death of Sir Wilfrid Laurier. May 1-June 15, Great strike at Winnipeg and other western cities. June 28, Signing at Versailles of Peace Treaty and Protocol. Aug. 15, Arrival of H.R.H. the Prince of Wales for official tour in Canada. Aug. 22, Formal opening of Quebec Bridge by H.R.H. the Prince of Wales. Sept. 1, H.R.H. the Prince of Wales lays foundation stone of tower of new Parliament Buildings at Ottawa.

1920. Jan. 10, Ratifications of the Treaty of Versailles. May 31-June 18, Trade Conference at Ottawa between Dominion and West Indian Governments. July 10, Sir Robert Borden is succeeded by Right Hon. Arthur Meighen as Premier. Nov. 15, First meeting of League of Nations Assembly begins at Geneva, Switzerland.

1921. June 20-August 5, Imperial Conference. Aug. 11, The Lord Byng of Vimy takes office as Governor-General. Nov. 11, Opening of Conference on limitation of armament at Washington. Dec. 6, Dominion general election. Dec. 29, New ministry (Liberal), with Right Hon. W. L. Mackenzie King as premier, is sworn in.

1922. Feb. 1, Arms Conference at Washington approves 5-power treaty limiting capital fighting ships and pledging against unrestricted submarine warfare and use of poison gas. Mar. 8, Opening of 14th Dominion Parliament.

1923. Sept. 3, Fourth session of League of Nations at Geneva. Oct. 1, Imperial Conference and Imperial Economic Conference at London.

1924. April 23, British Empire Exhibition opened by King George at Wembley, England, with the Prince of Wales as President. Sept. 1, Opening of fifth Session of League of Nations at Geneva, Switzerland.

1925. June 10, Inauguration of the United Church of Canada. July 6, Signing at Ottawa of trade agreement between Canada and the British West Indies. Oct. 29, Dominion general elections.

1926. April 15, Budget Speech; reductions of taxation announced. June 28, resignation of Twelfth Ministry of Right Hon. W. L. Mackenzie King. June 29, Right Hon. Arthur Meighen becomes Prime Minister. Sept. 14, Dominion General Elections. Sept. 25, Right Hon. W. L. Mackenzie King again becomes Prime Minister. Oct. 2, Lord Willingdon of Ratton takes office as Governor-General. Oct. 19-Nov. 23, Imperial Conference in London, England.

APPENDIX II

Statistical Summary of the Progress of Canada

Items		1871	1901	1911	1926
Population[1]—					
Prince Edward Island	No.	94,021	103,259	93,728	87,000
Nova Scotia	"	387,800	459,574	492,338	540,000
New Brunswick	"	285,594	331,120	351,889	407,200
Quebec	"	1,191,516	1,648,898	2,005,776	2,561,800
Ontario	"	1,620,851	2,182,947	2,527,292	3,145,600
Manitoba	"	25,228	255,211	461,394	639,000
Saskatchewan	"	–	91,279	492,432	821,000
Alberta	"	–	73,022	374,295	607,000
British Columbia	"	36,247	178,657	392,480	568,400
Yukon Territory	"	–	27,219	8,512	3,450
Northwest Territories	"	48,000	20,129	6,507	8,850
Canada	"	3,689,257	5,371,315	7,206,643	9,389,300
Immigration—					
From United Kingdom	No.	–	11,810	123,013	37,030
" United States	"	–	17,987	121,451	18,778
" Other Countries	"	–	19,352	66,620	40,256
Total	"	27,773	49,149	311,084	96,064
Agriculture—					
Area of occupied farms	acre	36,046,401	63,422,338	108,968,715	140,887,903[4]
Improved lands	"	17,335,818	30,166,033	48,733,823	70,769,548[4]
Field Crops—					
Wheat	acre	1,646,781	4,224,542	8,864,154	22,987,048
	bush.	16,723,873	55,572,368	132,077,547	409,811,000
	$	16,993,265	36,122,039	104,816,825	445,180,000
Oats	acre	–	5,367,655	8,656,179	12,741,057
	bush.	42,489,453	151,497,407	245,393,425	383,419,000
	$	15,966,310	51,509,118	86,796,130	184,108,000
Barley	acre	–	871,800	1,283,094	3,636,663
	bush.	11,496,038	22,224,366	28,848,310	99,684,100
	$	8,170,735	8,889,746	14,653,697	51,927,000
Corn	acre	–	360,758	293,951	209,725
	bush.	3,803,830	25,875,919	14,417,599	7,815,000
	$	2,883,145	11,902,923	5,774,039	7,780,000
Potatoes	acre	403,102	448,743	464,504	545,918
	bush.	47,330,187	55,362,635	55,461,478	48,682,000[3]
	$	15,211,774	13,842,658	27,426,765	71,598,000
Hay and Clover	acre	3,650,419	6,543,423	8,289,407	10,069,519
	ton	3,818,641	7,852,731	10,406,367	14,916,000
	$	38,869,900	85,625,315	90,115,531	178,526,000
Total Area Field Crops	acre	–	–	–	56,927,371
Total Value Field Crops	$	–	194,953,420	384,513,795	1,121,447,100
Live Stock[2]—					
Horses	No.	836,743	1,577,493	2,598,958	3,558,849
	$	–	118,279,419	381,915,505	254,675,000
Milch cows	No.	1,251,209	2,408,677	2,595,255	3,951,335
	$	–	69,237,970	109,575,526	205,816,000
Other Cattle	No.	1,373,081	3,167,174	3,930,828	5,208,815
	$	–	54,197,341	86,278,490	161,920,000
Sheep	No.	3,155,509	2,510,239	2,174,300	3,035,507
	$	–	10,490,594	10,701,691	30,273,000
Swine	No.	1,366,083	2,353,828	3,634,778	4,470,771
	$	–	16,445,702	26,986,621	71,971,000
Total value	$	–	268,651,026	615,457,833	724,655,000

[1] Estimated populations are given for 1926 except in the cases of the Prairie Provinces where there was a census in that year. [2] The figures for 1871-1911 are for the preceding years. [3] Cwt. [4] As ascertained at the census of 1921.

APPENDIX II—Continued
Statistical Summary of the Progress of Canada—Continued

Items		1871	1901	1911	1926[1]
Dairying[2]					
Cheese, factory	lb.	155,524	220,833,269	199,904,205	177,139,113
	$	17,585	22,221,430	21,587,124	36,571,556
Cheese, home-made	lb.	4,984,843	–	1,371,092	533,016
	$	573,257	–	154,088	95,073
Butter creamery	lb.	981,939	36,066,739	64,489,398	169,494,967
	$	188,532	7,240,972	15,597,807	63,008,097
Butter, home-made	lb.	74,190,584	105,343,076	137,110,200	100,000,000
	$	14,244,592	21,384,644	30,269,497	32,128,799
Miscellaneous dairy products	$	–	15,623,907	35,862,437	109,265,795
Total value of dairy products	$	15,023,966	66,470,953	103,381,854	241,069,320[3]
Fisheries[2]	$	7,573,199	25,737,153	34,667,872	47,942,131[3]
Raw Furs	$	–	899,645	1,927,550	14,905,588[3]
Minerals—					
Gold	oz.	105,187	1,167,216	473,159	1,748,364
	$	2,174,412	24,128,503	9,781,077	36,141,891
Silver	oz.	–	5,539,192	32,559,044	22,435,531
	$	–	3,265,354	17,355,272	13,934,035
Copper	lb.	–	37,827,019	55,648,011	132,345,152
	$	–	6,096,581	6,886,998	17,386,867
Lead	lb.	–	51,900,958	23,784,969	284,120,946
	$	–	2,249,387	827,717	19,262,242
Nickel	lb.	–	9,189,047	34,098,744	65,714,294
	$	–	4,594,523	10,229,623	14,374,163
Pig iron	ton	–	274,376	917,535	757,317
	$	–	3,512,923	12,307,125	16,660,974[4]
Coal	ton	1,063,742[5]	6,486,325	11,323,388	16,457,484
	$	1,763,423[5]	12,699,243	26,467,646	59,797,181
Cement	brl.	–	450,394	5,692,915	8,707,021
	$	–	660,030	7,644,537	13,013,283
Total value	$	–	65,797,911	103,220,994	241,245,898
Electric Statistics—					
Power Houses	No.	–	58	266	563[3]
Capital invested	$	–	11,891,025	110,838,746	726,721,087[3]
Kilowatt hours generated[6]	No.	–	–	–	10,110,459[3]
Subscribers	No.	–	–	–	1,279,731[3]
Turbine H.P. installed	No.	–	235,946	1,358,333	4,556,000[3]
Manufactures[7]—					
Employees	No.	187,942	339,173	515,203	544,014[3]
Capital	$	77,964,020	446,916,487	1,247,583,609	3,808,289,981[3]
Salaries and wages	$	40,851,009	113,249,350	241,008,416	596,015,171[3]
Products	$	221,617,773	481,053,375	1,165,975,639	2,948,545,315[3]
External Trade—					
Exports[8]	$	57,630,024	177,431,386	274,316,553	1,315,355,791
Imports[9]	$	84,214,388	177,930,919	452,724,603	927,328,732
Total	$	141,844,412	355,362,305	727,041,156	2,242,684,523
Exports to and Imports from U.K. and U.S.—					
Exports to United Kingdom	$	21,733,556	92,857,525	132,156,924	508,237,560
Imports from United Kingdom	$	48,498,202	42,820,334	109,934,753	163,731,210
Exports to United States	$	29,164,358	67,983,673	104,115,823	474,987,367
Imports from United States	$	27,185,586	107,377,906	275,824,265	609,719,637

[1] Or latest year. [2] The figures for 1871-1911 are for the preceding year. [3] 1925. [4] Estimated at $22 per long ton. [5] 1874. [6] 000's omitted. [7] The statistics of manufactures in 1871 include works employing fewer than 5 hands, while those for later years are for works employing 5 hands or over, except in the case of butter and cheese factories, flour and grist mills, electric light plants, lumber, lath and shingle mills, lime kilns, brick and tile works and fish canneries. The figures in each case are for the preceding years. For 1925 statistics are exclusive of construction, hand trades, repair and custom work. [8] Exports of domestic merchandise only. [9] Imports of merchandise for home consumption.

APPENDIX II—Continued
Statistical Summary of the Progress of Canada—Continued

Items		1871	1901	1911	1926
Exports, domestic, by chief items—					
Wheat	bush.	1,748,977	9,739,758	45,802,115	249,583,470
	$	1,981,917	6,871,939	45,521,134	364,201,388
Wheat flour	brl.	306,339	1,118,700	3,049,046	10,084,974
	$	1,609,849	4,015,226	13,854,790	69,687,598
Oats	bush.	542,386	8,155,063	5,431,662	43,058,283
	$	231,227	2,490,521	2,144,846	24,237,693
Hay	ton	23,487	252,977	326,132	368,787
	$	290,217	2,097,882	2,723,291	3,711,840
Bacon and hams, shoulders and sides.	cwt.	103,444	1,055,495	598,745	1,253,760
	$	1,018,918	11,778,446	8,526,332	28,590,301
Butter	lb.	15,439,266	16,335,528	3,142,682	23,303,865
	$	3,065,234	3,295,663	744,288	8,773,125
Cheese	lb.	8,271,439	195,926,697	181,895,724	148,333,500
	$	1,109,906	20,696,951	20,739,507	33,718,587
Gold	$	163,037	24,445,156	5,344,465	25,968,094
Silver	oz.	–	4,022,019	33,731,010	18,382,415
	$	595,261	2,420,750	17,269,168	12,365,576
Copper[1]	lb.	6,246,000	26,345,776	55,005,342	61,090,600
	$	120,121	2,659,261	5,575,033	7,037,206
Nickel	lb.	–	9,537,558	34,767,523	71,081,400
	$	–	958,365	3,842,332	12,829,244
Coal	ton	318,287	1,888,538	2,315,171	753,842
	$	662,451	5,307,060	6,014,095	4,083,713
Asbestos	ton	–	26,715	69,829	269,652
	$	–	864,573	2,076,477	9,920,900
Wood pulp	cwt.	–	–	6,588,655	19,812,381
	$	–	1,937,207	5,715,532	49,909,870
Newsprint paper	cwt.	–	–	–	29,537,366
	$	–	–	3,092,437	102,238,568
Exports, domestic, by classes—					
Vegetable products (except chemicals, fibres and wood)	$	–	25,541,567	84,556,886	606,058,672
Animals and their products (except chemicals and fibres)	$	–	68,465,332	69,693,263	190,975,417
Fibres, textiles and textile products	$	–	1,880,539	1,818,931	8,940,046
Wood, wood products and paper	$	–	33,099,915	56,334,695	278,674,960
Iron and its products	$	–	3,778,897	9,884,346	74,735,077
Non-ferrous metals and their products	$	–	33,395,096	34,000,996	97,476,270
Non-metallic minerals and their products	$	–	7,356,324	10,038,493	24,568,845
Chemicals and allied products	$	–	791,975	2,900,379	17,498,128
All other commodities	$	–	3,121,741	5,088,564	16,428,376
Total exports, domestic.	$	57,630,024	177,431,386	274,316,553	1,315,355,791
Imports for Consumption—					
Vegetable products (except chemicals, fibres and wood)	$	–	38,036,757	79,214,342	203,417,431
Animals and their products (except chemicals and fibres)	$	–	14,022,896	30,671,908	49,185,558
Fibres, textiles and textile products	$	–	37,284,752	87,916,282	184,761,831
Wood, wood products and paper	$	–	8,196,901	26,851,936	40,403,096
Iron and its products	$	–	29,955,936	91,968,180	181,196,800
Non-ferrous metals and their products	$	–	7,159,142	27,655,874	47,692,985
Non-metallic minerals and their products (except chemicals)	$	–	21,255,403	53,335,826	139,033,940

[1] Copper, fine, contained in ore, matte, regulus, etc.

APPENDIX II—Continued

Statistical Summary of the Progress of Canada—Continued

Items		1871	1901	1911	1926[3]
Chemicals and allied products	$	–	5,692,564	12,489,776	28,404,276
All other commodities	$	–	16,326,568	42,620,479	53,232,815
Total imports	$	84,214,388	177,930,919	452,724,603	927,328,732
Steam Railways—					
Miles in operation	No.	2,695	18,140	25,400	40,352[4]
Capital	$	257,035,188[1]	816,110,837	1,528,689,201	3,471,080,909[4]
Passengers	No.	5,190,416[2]	18,385,722	37,097,718	41,458,084[4]
Freight	ton	5,670,836[2]	36,999,371	79,884,282	109,850,925[4]
Earnings	$	19,470,539[2]	72,898,749	188,733,494	455,297,288[4]
Expenses	$	15,775,532[2]	50,368,726	131,034,785	372,149,656[4]
Electric Railways—					
Miles in operation	No.	–	675	1,224	1,738[4]
Capital	$	–	–	111,532,347	221,769,220[4]
Passengers	No.	–	120,934,656	426,296,792	725,491,101[4]
Freight	ton	–	287,926	1,228,362	2,706,312[4]
Earnings	$	–	5,768,283	20,356,952	49,626,231[4]
Expenses	$	–	3,435,162	12,096,134	35,426,487[4]
Canals—					
Passengers carried	No.	100,377	190,428	304,904	197,561
Freight	ton	3,955,621	5,665,259	38,030,353	13,477,663
Shipping (Sea-going)—					
Entered	ton	2,521,573	7,514,732	11,919,339	22,837,720
Cleared	"	2,594,460	7,028,330	10,377,847	22,817,276
Total	"	5,116,033	14,543,062	22,297,186	45,654,996
Shipping (Inland International)—					
Entered	ton	4,055,198	5,720,575	13,286,102	14,117,099
Cleared	"	3,954,797	5,766,171	11,846,257	15,474,732
Total	"	8,009,995	11,486,746	25,132,359	29,591,831
Shipping (Coastwise)—					
Entered	ton	–	17,927,959	34,280,669	41,770,480
Cleared	"	–	16,516,832	32,347,265	41,117,175
Total	"	–	34,444,796	66,627,934	82,887,655
Telegraphs, Government, miles of line		–	5,744	8,446	10,721[4]
Telegraphs, other, miles of line		–	30,194	33,905	42,042[4]
Telephones	No.	–	63,192	302,759	1,144,095[4]
Motor vehicles	"	–	–	21,519	836,794
Post Office—					
Revenue	$	803,637	3,421,192	9,146,952	31,024,464
Expenditure	$	994,876	3,837,376	7,954,223	30,732,423
Money orders issued	$	4,546,434	17,956,258	70,614,862	177,840,231
Dominion Finance—					
Customs Revenue	$	11,841,105	28,293,930	71,838,089	127,355,143
Excise Revenue	$	4,295,945	10,318,266	16,869,837	42,923,549
Total Ordinary Revenue	$	19,335,561	52,514,701	117,780,409	380,745,506
Revenue per head	$	5·50	9·72	16·34	40·06
Total Ordinary Expenditure	$	15,623,082	46,866,368	87,774,198	320,660,479
Expenditure per head	$	4·44	8·67	12·18	33·74
Total Disbursements	$	19,293,478	57,982,866	122,861,250	355,186,423
Disbursements per head	$	5·48	10·73	17·04	37·37
Gross debt	$	115,492,683	354,732,433	474,941,487	2,768,779,184
Assets	$	37,786,165	86,252,429	134,899,435	379,048,085[5]
Net debt	$	77,706,518	268,480,004	340,042,052	2,389,731,099

[1]Year 1876. [2]Year 1875. [3]Or latest year. [4]1925. [5]Active assets only.

APPENDIX II—Concluded

Statistical Summary of the Progress of Canada—Concluded

Items		1871	1901	1911	1926[4]
Provincial Finance—					
Revenue, Ordinary, Total...	$	6,090,783[1]	14,074,991	40,706,948	132,398,729[5]
Expenditure, Ordinary,Total	$	5,180,872[1]	14,146,059	38,144,511	136,648,242[5]
Note Circulation—					
Bank Notes.................	$	20,914,637	50,601,205	89,982,223	168,885,995
Dominion Notes...........	$	7,244,341[6]	27,898,509[5]	99,921,354	190,004,824
Chartered Banks—					
Capital paid-up..............	$	37,095,340	67,035,615	103,009,256	116,638,254
Assets.....................	$	125,273,631	531,829,324	1,303,131,260	2,864,019,213
Liabilities (excluding capital and reserves)..............	$	80,250,974	420,003,743	1,097,661,393	2,604,601,786
Deposits payable on demand	$	–	95,169,631	304,801,755	553,322,935
Deposits payable after notice	$	–	221,624,664	568,976,209	1,340,559,021
Total deposits[2]...........	$	56,287,391	349,573,327	980,433,788	2,277,192,043
Savings Banks—					
Deposits in Post Office......	$	2,497,260	39,950,813	43,330,579	24,035,669
Government................	$	2,072,037	16,098,144	14,673,752	8,794,875
Special.....................	$	5,766,712	19,125,097	34,770,386	67,241,344
Loan Companies[3]—					
Assets.....................	$	8,392,464	158,523,307	389,701,988	110,638,667[5]
Liabilities to shareholders and public................	$	8,392,464	158,523,307	389,701,988	109,527,773[5]
Deposits...................	$	2,399,136	20,756,910	33,742,513	18,660,122[5]
Dominion Fire Insurance—					
Amount at risk, Dec. 31.....	$	228,453,784	1,038,687,619	2,279,868,346	8,045,437,096[7]
Premium income for year...	$	2,321,716	9,650,348	20,575,255	52,573,001[7]
Dominion Life Insurance—					
Amount at risk, Dec. 31....	$	45,825,935	463,769,034	950,220,771	4,609,902,248[7]
Premium income for year...	$	1,852,974	15,189,854	31,619,626	146,583,956[7]
Education in Day Schools—					
Enrolment..................	No.	–	1,083,000	1,356,879	1,965,632[5]
Average daily attendance....	"	–	669,000	870,801	1,517,250[5]
No. of Teachers............	"	13,559	27,126	40,516	62,394[5]
Total Public Expenditure....	$	–	11,044,925	37,971,374	121,034,234[5]

[1]Average, 1869-1872. [2]Including amounts deposited elsewhere than in Canada from 1901-1926. [3]Including Building Societies and Trust Companies (1871-1911). [4]Or latest year. [5] 1925. [6] As at June 30. [7] Figures subject to revision.

NOTE

In the foregoing Summary, the statistics of immigration, fisheries (1871-1916), trade, shipping, the Post Office, the public debt, revenue and expenditure and the Post Office and Government Savings Banks relate to the fiscal years ended June 30 up to 1906, and from that on to the years ended March 31. Agricultural, dairying, fisheries (1921-25), mineral, manufacturing, banking, insurance, loan and trust companies statistics relate to the calendar years and railway statistics to the years ended June 30, 1871-1916, and to the calendar years 1921-1925. Canal statistics are those of the navigation seasons. The telegraph statistics relate to the fiscal years for Government lines and to the calendar years for other lines.

APPENDIX III

NOTE.—For purposes of historical reference the text of the original British North America Act, 1867, is printed herewith. Since Confederation no fewer than thirty-three Acts have been passed by the Parliament of the United Kingdom modifying the original Act, together with four Orders-in-Council. These deal with the admission of new provinces, the extension of the boundaries of various provinces, the amendments of the financial terms of Confederation, etc. These will be found republished in a volume entitled "British North America Acts, 1867-1919", published by the King's Printer, Ottawa, 1919.

THE BRITISH NORTH AMERICA ACT, 1867.
30 VICTORIA, CHAPTER 3.

An Act for the Union of Canada, Nova Scotia, and New Brunswick, and the Government thereof; and for Purposes connected therewith.

[29*th March*, 1867.]

WHEREAS the Provinces of Canada, Nova Scotia, and New Brunswick have expressed their Desire to be federally united into One Dominion under the Crown of the United Kingdom of Great Britain and Ireland, with a Constitution similar in Principle to that of the United Kingdom:

And whereas such a Union would conduce to the Welfare of the Provinces and promote the Interests of the British Empire:

And whereas on the Establishment of the Union by Authority of Parliament it is expedient, not only that the Constitution of the Legislative Authority in the Dominion be provided for, but also that the Nature of the Executive Government therein be declared:

And whereas it is expedient that Provision be made for the eventual admission into the Union of other parts of British North America:

Be it therefore enacted and declared by the Queen's most Excellent Majesty, by and with the Advice and Consent of the Lords Spiritual and Temporal, and Commons, in this present Parliament assembled, and by the Authority of the same, as follows:

I.—PRELIMINARY.

1. This Act may be cited as The British North America Act, 1867.

Short Title.

2. The Provisions of this Act referring to Her Majesty the Queen extend also to the Heirs and Successors of Her Majesty, Kings and Queens of the United Kingdom of Great Britain and Ireland.

Application of Provisions referring to the Queen.

II.—UNION.

3. It shall be lawful for the Queen, by and with the Advice of Her Majesty's Most Honourable Privy Council, to declare by Proclamation that, on and after a Day therein appointed,

Declaration of Union.

141

not being more than Six Months after the passing of this Act, the Provinces of Canada, Nova Scotia, and New Brunswick shall form and be One Dominion under the Name of Canada; and on and after that Day those Three Provinces shall form and be One Dominion under that Name accordingly.

Construction of subsequent Provisions of Act.

4. The subsequent Provisions of this Act shall, unless it is otherwise expressed or implied, commence and have effect on and after the Union, that is to say, on and after the Day appointed for the Union taking effect in the Queen's Proclamation; and in the same Provisions, unless it is otherwise expressed or implied, the Name Canada shall be taken to mean Canada as constituted under this Act.

Four Provinces.

5. Canada shall be divided into Four Provinces, named Ontario, Quebec, Nova Scotia, and New Brunswick.

Provinces of Ontario and Quebec.

6. The Parts of the Province of Canada (as it exists at the passing of this Act) which formerly constituted respectively the Provinces of Upper Canada and Lower Canada shall be deemed to be severed, and shall form two separate Provinces. The Part which formerly constituted the Province of Upper Canada shall constitute the Province of Ontario; and the Part which formerly constituted the Province of Lower Canada shall constitute the Province of Quebec.

Provinces of Nova Scotia and New Brunswick.

Decennial Census.

7. The Provinces of Nova Scotia and New Brunswick shall have the same Limits as at the passing of this Act.

8. In the general Census of the Population of Canada which is hereby required to be taken in the Year One thousand eight hundred and seventy-one, and in every Tenth Year thereafter, the respective Populations of the Four Provinces shall be distinguished.

III.—EXECUTIVE POWER.

Declaration of Executive Power in the Queen.

9. The Executive Government and Authority of and over Canada is hereby declared to continue and be vested in the Queen.

Application of Provisions referring to Governor General.

10. The Provisions of this Act referring to the Governor General extend and apply to the Governor General for the Time being of Canada, or other the Chief Executive Officer or Administrator for the Time being carrying on the Government of Canada on behalf and in the Name of the Queen, by whatever Title he is designated.

Constitution of Privy Council for Canada.

11. There shall be a Council to aid and advise in the Government of Canada, to be styled the Queen's Privy Council for Canada; and the Persons who are to be Members of that Council shall be from Time to Time chosen and summoned by the Governor General and sworn in as Privy Councillors, and Members thereof may be from Time to Time removed by the Governor General.

All Powers under Acts to be exercised by Governor General with advice of Privy Council or alone.

12. All Powers, Authorities, and Functions which under any Act of the Parliament of Great Britain, or of the Parliament of the United Kingdom of Great Britain and Ireland, or of the Legislature of Upper Canada, Lower Canada, Canada, Nova Scotia, or New Brunswick, are at the Union vested in or exerciseable by the respective Governors or Lieutenant Governors of those Provinces, with the Advice, or with the Advice and Consent, of the respective Executive Councils thereof, or in conjunction with those Councils, or with any Number of Members thereof, or by those Governors or Lieutenant Governors individually, shall, as far as the same continue in existence and capable of being exercised after the Union in relation to the Government of Canada, be vested in and exerciseable by the Governor General, with the Advice or with the Advice and Consent of or in conjunction with the Queen's Privy Council for Canada, or any Members thereof, or by the Governor General individually, as the Case requires, subject nevertheless (except with respect to such as exist under Acts of the Parliament of Great Britain or of the Parliament of the United Kingdom of Great Britain and Ireland) to be abolished or altered by the Parliament of Canada.

13. The Provisions of this Act referring to the Governor General in Council shall be construed as referring to the Governor General acting by and with the Advice of the Queen's Privy Council for Canada. *Application of Provisions referring to Governor General in Council.*

14. It shall be lawful for the Queen, if Her Majesty thinks fit, to authorize the Governor General from Time to Time to appoint any Person or any Persons jointly or severally to be his Deputy or Deputies within any Part or Parts of Canada, and in that Capacity to exercise during the Pleasure of the Governor General such of the Powers, Authorities, and Functions of the Governor General as the Governor General deems it necessary or expedient to assign to him or them, subject to any Limitations or Directions expressed or given by the Queen; but the Appointment of such a Deputy or Deputies shall not affect the Exercise by the Governor General himself of any Power, Authority, or Function. *Power to Her Majesty to authorize Governor General to appoint Deputies.*

15. The Command-in-Chief of the Land and Naval Militia, and of all Naval and Military Forces, of and in Canada, is hereby declared to continue and be vested in the Queen. *Command of Armed Forces to continue to be vested in the Queen.*

16. Until the Queen otherwise directs the Seat of Government of Canada shall be Ottawa. *Seat of Government of Canada.*

IV.—LEGISLATIVE POWER.

17. There shall be One Parliament for Canada, consisting of the Queen, an Upper House styled the Senate, and the House of Commons. *Constitution of Parliament of Canada.*

18. The Privileges, Immunities, and Powers to be held, enjoyed, and exercised by the Senate and by the House of Commons and by the Members thereof respectively shall be such as are from Time to Time defined by Act of the Parliament of Canada, but so that the same shall never exceed those at the passing of this Act held, enjoyed, and exercised by the Commons House of Parliament of the United Kingdom of Great Britain and Ireland and by the Members thereof. *Privileges, &c., of Houses.*

19. The Parliament of Canada shall be called together not later than Six Months after the Union. *First Session of the Parliament of Canada.*

20. There shall be a Session of the Parliament of Canada once at least in every Year, so that Twelve Months shall not intervene between the last Sitting of the Parliament in one Session and its first Sitting in the next Session. *Yearly Session of the Parliament of Canada.*

143

The Senate.

Number of Senators.

21. The Senate shall, subject to the Provisions of this Act, consist of Seventy-two Members, who shall be styled Senators.

Representation of Provinces in Senate.

22. In relation to the Constitution of the Senate, Canada shall be deemed to consist of Three Divisions:

1. Ontario;
2. Quebec;
3. The Maritime Provinces, Nova Scotia and New Brunswick; which Three Divisions shall (subject to the Provisions of this Act) be equally represented in the Senate as follows: Ontario by Twenty-four Senators; Quebec by Twenty-four Senators; and the Maritime Provinces by Twenty-four Senators, Twelve thereof representing Nova Scotia, and Twelve thereof representing New Brunswick.

In the Case of Quebec each of the Twenty-four Senators representing that Province shall be appointed for One of the Twenty-four Electoral Divisions of Lower Canada specified in Schedule A. to Chapter One of the Consolidated Statutes of Canada.

Qualifications of Senator.

23. The Qualifications of a Senator shall be as follows:
(1.) He shall be of the full age of Thirty Years:
(2.) He shall be either a Natural-born Subject of the Queen, or a Subject of the Queen naturalized by an Act of the Parliament of Great Britain, or of the Parliament of the United Kingdom of Great Britain and Ireland, or of the Legislature of One of the Provinces of Upper Canada, Lower Canada, Canada, Nova Scotia, or New Brunswick, before the Union, or of the Parliament of Canada after the Union:
(3.) He shall be legally or equitably seised as of Freehold for his own Use and Benefit of Lands or Tenements held in free and common Socage, or seised or possessed for his own Use and Benefit of Lands or Tenements held in Franc-alleu or in Roture, within the Province for which he is appointed, of the Value of Four thousand Dollars, over and above all Rents, Dues, Debts, Charges, Mortgages, and Incumbrances due or payable out of or charged on or affecting the same:
(4.) His Real and Personal Property shall be together worth Four thousand Dollars over and above his Debts and Liabilities:
(5.) He shall be resident in the Province for which he is appointed:
(6.) In the case of Quebec he shall have his Real Property Qualification in the Electoral Division for which he is appointed, or shall be resident in that Division.

Summons of Senator.

24. The Governor General shall from Time to Time, in the Queen's Name, by Instrument under the Great Seal of Canada, summon qualified Persons to the Senate; and, subject to the Provisions of this Act, every Person so summoned shall become and be a Member of the Senate and a Senator.

Summons of First Body of Senators.

25. Such Persons shall be first summoned to the Senate as the Queen by Warrant under Her Majesty's Royal Sign Manual thinks fits to approve, and their Names shall be inserted in the Queen's Proclamation of Union.

Addition of Senators in certain cases.

26. If at any Time on the Recommendation of the Governor General the Queen thinks fit to direct that Three or Six Members be added to the Senate, the Governor General may by Summons to Three or Six qualified Persons (as the Case may be), representing equally the Three Divisions of Canada, add to the Senate accordingly.

27. In case of such Addition being at any Time made the Governor General shall not summon any Person to the Senate, except on a further like Direction by the Queen on the like Recommendation, until each of the Three Divisions of Canada is represented by Twenty-four Senators and no more. Reduction of Senate to normal number.

28. The Number of Senators shall not at any Time exceed Seventy-eight. Maximum number of Senators.

29. A Senator shall, subject to the Provisions of this Act, hold his Place in the Senate for Life. Tenure of Place in Senate.

30. A Senator may by Writing under his Hand addressed to the Governor General resign his Place in the Senate, and thereupon the same shall be vacant. Resignation of Place in Senate.

31. The Place of a Senator shall become vacant in any of the following Cases:— Disqualification of Senators.

(1.) If for Two consecutive Sessions of the Parliament he fails to give his Attendance in the Senate:

(2.) If he takes an Oath or makes a Declaration or Acknowledgment of Allegiance, Obedience, or Adherence to a Foreign Power, or does an Act whereby he becomes a Subject or Citizen, or entitled to the Rights or Privileges of a Subject or Citizen, of a Foreign Power:

(3.) If he is adjudged Bankrupt or Insolvent, or applies for the Benefit of any Law relating to Insolvent Debtors, or becomes a public Defaulter:

(4.) It he is attainted of Treason or convicted of Felony or of any infamous Crime:

(5.) If he ceases to be qualified in respect of Property or of Residence; provided, that a Senator shall not be deemed to have ceased to be qualified in respect of Residence by reason only of his residing at the Seat of the Government of Canada while holding an Office under that Government requiring his Presence there.

32. When a vacancy happens in the Senate by Resignation, Death, or otherwise, the Governor General shall by Summons to a fit and qualified Person fill the Vacancy. Summons on Vacancy in Senate.

33. If any Question arises respecting the Qualification of a Senator or a Vacancy in the Senate the same shall be heard and determined by the Senate. Questions as to Qualifications and Vacancies in Senate.

34. The Governor General may from Time to Time, by Instrument under the Great Seal of Canada, appoint a Senator to be Speaker of the Senate, and may remove him and appoint another in his Stead. Appointment of Speaker of Senate.

35. Until the Parliament of Canada otherwise provides, the Presence of at least Fifteen Senators, including the Speaker, shall be necessary to constitute a Meeting of the Senate for the Exercise of its Powers. Quorum of Senate.

36. Questions arising in the Senate shall be decided by a Majority of Voices, and the Speaker shall in all Cases have a Vote, and when the Voices are equal the Decision shall be deemed to be in the Negative. Voting in Senate.

The House of Commons.

Constitution of House of Commons in Canada.

37. The House of Commons shall, subject to the Provisions of this Act, consist of One hundred and eighty-one Members, of whom Eighty-two shall be elected for Ontario, Sixty-five for Quebec, Nineteen for Nova Scotia, and Fifteen for New Brunswick.

Summoning of House of Commons.

38. The Governor General shall from Time to Time, in the Queen's Name, by Instrument under the Great Seal of Canada, summon and call together the House of Commons.

Senators not to sit in House of Commons.

39. A Senator shall not be capable of being elected or of sitting or voting as a Member of the House of Commons.

Electoral districts of the four Provinces.

40. Until the Parliament of Canada otherwise provides, Ontario, Quebec, Nova Scotia, and New Brunswick shall, for the Purposes of the Election of Members to serve in the House of Commons, be divided into Electoral Districts as follows:

1.—Ontario.

Ontario shall be divided into the Counties, Ridings of Counties, Cities, Parts of Cities, and Towns enumerated in the First Schedule to this Act, each whereof shall be an Electoral District, each such District as numbered in that Schedule being entitled to return One Member.

2.—Quebec.

Quebec shall be divided into Sixty-five Electoral Districts, composed of the Sixty-five Electoral Divisions into which Lower Canada is at the passing of this Act divided under Chapter Two of the Consolidated Statutes of Canada, Chapter Seventy-five of the Consolidated Statutes for Lower Canada, and the Act of the Province of Canada of the Twenty-third Year of the Queen, Chapter One, or any other Act amending the same in force at the Union, so that each such Electoral Division shall be for the Purposes of this Act an Electoral District entitled to return One Member.

3.—Nova Scotia.

Each of the Eighteen Counties of Nova Scotia shall be an Electoral District. The County of Halifax shall be entitled to return Two Members, and each of the other Counties One Member.

4.—New Brunswick.

Each of the Fourteen Counties into which New Brunswick is divided, including the City and County of St. John, shall be an Electoral District. The City of St. John shall be a separate Electoral District. Each of those Fifteen Electoral Districts shall be entitled to return One Member.

Continuance of existing Election Laws until Parliament of Canada otherwise provides.

41. Until the Parliament of Canada otherwise provides, all Laws in force in the several Provinces at the Union relative to the following Matters or any of them, namely,—the Qualifications and Disqualifications of Persons to be elected or to sit or vote as Members of the House of Assembly or Legislative Assembly in the several Provinces, the Voters at Elections of such Members, the Oaths to be taken by Voters, the Returning Officers, their Powers and Duties, the Proceedings at Elections, the Periods during which Elections may be continued, the Trial of controverted Elections, and Proceedings incident thereto, the vacating of Seats of Members, and the Execution of new Writs in case of Seats vacated otherwise than by Dissolution,—shall respectively apply to Elections of Members to serve in the House of Commons for the same several Provinces.

Provided that, until the Parliament of Canada otherwise provides, at any Election for a Member of the House of Commons for the District of Algoma, in addition to Persons qualified by the Law of the Province of Canada to vote, every male British Subject, aged Twenty-one Years or upwards, being a Householder, shall have a Vote.

42. For the First Election of Members to serve in the House of Commons the Governor General shall cause Writs to be issued by such Person, in such Form, and addressed to such Returning Officers as he thinks fit. *Writs for first Election.*

The Person issuing Writs under this Section shall have the like Powers as are possessed at the Union by the Officers charged with the issuing of Writs for the Election of Members to serve in the respective House of Assembly or Legislative Assembly of the Province of Canada, Nova Scotia, or New Brunswick; and the Returning Officers to whom Writs are directed under this Section shall have the like Powers as are possessed at the Union by the Officers charged with the returning of Writs for the Election of Members to serve in the same respective House of Assembly or Legislative Assembly.

43. In case a Vacancy in the Representation in the House of Commons of any Electoral District happens before the Meeting of the Parliament, or after the Meeting of the Parliament before Provision is made by the Parliament in this Behalf, the Provisions of the last foregoing Section of this Act shall extend and apply to the issuing and returning of a Writ in respect of such vacant District. *As to casual Vacancies.*

44. The House of Commons on its first assembling after a General Election shall proceed with all practicable Speed to elect One of its Members to be Speaker. *As to Election of Speaker of House of Commons.*

45. In case of a Vacancy happening in the Office of Speaker by Death, Resignation, or otherwise, the House of Commons shall with all practicable Speed proceed to elect another of its Members to be Speaker. *As to filling up Vacancy in Office of Speaker.*

46. The Speaker shall preside at all Meetings of the House of Commons. *Speaker to preside.*

47. Until the Parliament of Canada otherwise provides, in case of the Absence for any Reason of the Speaker from the Chair of the House of Commons for a period of Forty-eight consecutive Hours, the House may elect another of its Members to act as Speaker, and the Member so elected shall during the Continuance of such Absence of the Speaker have and execute all the Powers, Privileges, and Duties of Speaker. *Provision in case of absence of Speaker.*

48. The Presence of at least Twenty Members of the House of Commons shall be necessary to constitute a Meeting of the House for the Exercise of its Powers; and for that Purpose the Speaker shall be reckoned as a Member. *Quorum of House of Commons.*

49. Questions arising in the House of Commons shall be decided by a Majority of Voices other than that of the Speaker, and when the Voices are equal, but not otherwise, the Speaker shall have a Vote. *Voting in House of Commons.*

Duration of House of Commons.

50. Every House of Commons shall continue for Five Years from the Day of the Return of the Writs for choosing the House (subject to be sooner dissolved by the Governor General), and no longer.

Decennial Re-adjustment of Representation.

51. On the Completion of the Census in the Year One thousand eight hundred and seventy-one, and of each subsequent decennial Census, the Representation of the Four Provinces shall be re-adjusted by such Authority, in such Manner, and from such Time, as the Parliament of Canada from Time to Time provides, subject and according to the following Rules:

(1.) Quebec shall have the fixed Number of Sixty-five Members:

(2.) There shall be assigned to each of the other Provinces such a Number of Members as will bear the same Proportion to the Number of its Population (ascertained at such Census) as the Number Sixty-five bears to the Number of the Population of Quebec (so ascertained):

(3.) In the Computation of the Number of Members for a Province a fractional Part not exceeding One Half of the whole Number requisite for entitling the Province to a Member shall be disregarded; but a fractional Part exceeding One Half of that Number shall be equivalent to the whole Number:

(4.) On any such Re-adjustment the Number of Members for a Province shall not be reduced unless the Proportion which the Number of the Population of the Province bore to the Number of the aggregate Population of Canada at the then last preceding Re-adjustment of the Number of Members for the Province is ascertained at the then latest Census to be diminished by One Twentieth Part or upwards:

(5.) Such Re-adjustment shall not take effect until the Termination of the then existing Parliament.

Increase of number of House of Commons.

52. The Number of Members of the House of Commons may be from Time to Time increased by the Parliament of Canada, provided the proportionate Representation of the Provinces prescribed by this Act is not thereby disturbed.

Money Votes; Royal Assent.

Appropriation and tax Bills.

53. Bills for appropriating any Part of the Public Revenue or for imposing any Tax or Impost, shall originate in the House of Commons.

Recommendation of money votes.

54. It shall not be lawful for the House of Commons to adopt or pass any Vote, Resolution, Address, or Bill for the Appropriation of any Part of the Public Revenue, or of any Tax or Impost, to any Purpose that has not been first recommended to that House by Message of the Governor General in the Session in which such Vote, Resolution, Address, or Bill is proposed.

Royal Assent to Bills, &c.

55. Where a Bill passed by the Houses of the Parliament is presented to the Governor General for the Queen's Assent, he shall declare, according to his Discretion, but subject to the Provisions of this Act and to Her Majesty's Instructions, either that he assents thereto in the Queen's Name, or that he withholds the Queen's Assent, or that he reserves the Bill for the Signification of the Queen's Pleasure.

56. Where the Governor General assents to a Bill in the Queen's Name, he shall by the first convenient Opportunity send an authentic Copy of the Act to one of Her Majesty's Principal Secretaries of State, and if the Queen in Council within Two Years after Receipt thereof by the Secretary of State thinks fit to disallow the Act, such Disallowance (with a Certificate of the Secretary of State of the Day on which the Act was received by him) being signified by the Governor General, by Speech or Message to each of the Houses of the Parliament or by Proclamation, shall annul the Act from and after the Day of such Signification.

Disallowance by order in Council of Act assented to by Governor General.

57. A Bill reserved for the Signification of the Queen's Pleasure shall not have any Force unless and until within Two Years from the Day on which it was presented to the Governor General for the Queen's Assent, the Governor General signifies, by Speech or Message to each of the Houses of the Parliament or by Proclamation, that it has received the Assent of the Queen in Council.

An Entry of every such Speech, Message, or Proclamation shall be made in the Journal of each House, and a Duplicate thereof duly attested shall be delivered to the proper Officer to be kept among the Records of Canada.

Signification of Queen's pleasure on Bill reserved.

V.—PROVINCIAL CONSTITUTIONS.

Executive Power.

58. For each Province there shall be an Officer, styled the Lieutenant Governor, appointed by the Governor General in Council by Instrument under the Great Seal of Canada.

Appointment of Lieutenant Governors of Provinces.

59. A Lieutenant Governor shall hold Office during the Pleasure of the Governor General; but any Lieutenant Governor appointed after the Commencement of the First Session of the Parliament of Canada shall not be removable within Five Years from his Appointment, except for Cause assigned, which shall be communicated to him in Writing within One Month after the Order for his Removal is made, and shall be communicated by Message to the Senate and to the House of Commons within One Week thereafter if the Parliament is then sitting, and if not then within One Week after the Commencement of the next Session of the Parliament.

Tenure of office of Lieutenant Governor.

60. The Salaries of the Lieutenant Governors shall be fixed and provided by the Parliament of Canada.

Salaries of Lieutenant Governors.

61. Every Lieutenant Governor shall, before assuming the Duties of his Office, make and subscribe before the Governor General or some Person authorized by him, Oaths of Allegiance and Office similar to those taken by the Governor General.

Oaths, &c., of Lieutenant Governor.

62. The Provisions of this Act referring to the Lieutenant Governor extend and apply to the Lieutenant Governor for the Time being of each Province or other the Chief Executive Officer or Administrator for the Time being carrying on the Government of the Province, by whatever Title he is designated.

Application of provisions referring to Lieutenant Governor.

63. The Executive Council of Ontario and of Quebec shall be composed of such Persons as the Lieutenant Governor from Time to Time thinks fit, and in the first instance of the following Officers, namely,—the Attorney General, the Secretary and

Appointment of Executive Officers for Ontario and Quebec.

149

Registrar of the Province, the Treasurer of the Province, the Commissioner of Crown Lands, and the Commissioner of Agriculture and Public Works, with in Quebec, the Speaker of the Legislative Council and the Solicitor General.

Executive Government of Nova Scotia and New Brunswick.

64. The Constitution of the Executive Authority in each of the Provinces of Nova Scotia and New Brunswick shall, subject to the Provisions of this Act, continue as it exists at the Union until altered under the Authority of this Act.

Powers to be exercised by Lieutenant Governor of Ontario or Quebec with advice or alone.

65. All Powers, Authorities, and Functions which under any Act of the Parliament of Great Britain, or of the Parliament of the United Kingdom of Great Britain and Ireland, or of the Legislature of Upper Canada, Lower Canada, or Canada, were or are before or at the Union vested in or exerciseable by the respective Governors or Lieutenant Governors of those Provinces, with the Advice or with the Advice and Consent of the respective Executive Councils thereof, or in conjunction with those Councils, or with any Number of Members thereof, or by those Governors or Lieutenant Governors individually, shall, as far as the same are capable of being exercised after the Union in relation to the Government of Ontario and Quebec respectively, be vested in and shall or may be exercised by the Lieutenant Governor of Ontario and Quebec respectively, with the Advice or with the Advice and Consent of or in conjunction with the respective Executive Councils, or any Members thereof, or by the Lieutenant Governor individually, as the Case requires, subject nevertheless (except with respect to such as exist under Acts of the Parliament of Great Britain, or of the Parliament of the United Kingdom of Great Britain and Ireland,) to be abolished or altered by the respective Legislatures of Ontario and Quebec.

Application of provisions referring to Lieutenant Governor in Council.

66. The Provisions of this Act referring to the Lieutenant Governor in Council shall be construed as referring to the Lieutenant Governor of the Province acting by and with the Advice of the Executive Council thereof.

Administration in absence, &c., of Lieutenant Governor.

67. The Governor General in Council may from Time to Time appoint an Administrator to execute the Office and Functions of Lieutenant Governor during his Absence, Illness, or other Inability.

Seats of Provincial Governments.

68. Unless and until the Executive Government of any Province otherwise directs with respect to that Province, the Seats of Government of the Provinces shall be as follows, namely,—of Ontario, the City of Toronto; of Quebec, the City of Quebec; of Nova Scotia, the City of Halifax; and of New Brunswick, the City of Fredericton.

Legislative Power.

1. —ONTARIO.

Legislature for Ontario.

69. There shall be a Legislature for Ontario consisting of the Lieutenant Governor and of One House, styled the Legislative Assembly of Ontario.

Electoral districts.

70. The Legislative Assembly of Ontario shall be composed of Eighty-two Members, to be elected to represent the Eighty-two Electoral Districts set forth in the First Schedule to this Act.

2.—QUEBEC.

71. There shall be a Legislature for Quebec consisting of the Lieutenant-Governor and of Two Houses, styled the Legislative Council of Quebec and the Legislative Assembly of Quebec. *Legislature for Quebec.*

72. The Legislative Council of Quebec shall be composed of Twenty-four Members, to be appointed by the Lieutenant Governor, in the Queen's Name, by Instrument under the Great Seal of Quebec, one being appointed to represent each of the Twenty-four Electoral Divisions of Lower Canada in this Act referred to, and each holding Office for the Term of his Life, unless the Legislature of Quebec otherwise provides under the Provisions of this Act. *Constitution of Legislative Council.*

73. The Qualifications of the Legislative Councillors of Quebec shall be the same as those of the Senators for Quebec. *Qualification of Legislative Councillors.*

74. The Place of a Legislative Councillor of Quebec shall become vacant in the Cases, *mutatis mutandis*, in which the Place of Senator becomes vacant. *Resignation, Disqualification, &c.*

75. When a Vacancy happens in the Legislative Council of Quebec by Resignation, Death, or otherwise, the Lieutenant Governor, in the Queen's Name, by Instrument under the Great Seal of Quebec, shall appoint a fit and qualified Person to fill the Vacancy. *Vacancies.*

76. If any Question arises respecting the Qualification of a Legislative Councillor of Quebec, or a Vacancy in the Legislative Council of Quebec, the same shall be heard and determined by the Legislative Council. *Questions as to Vacancies, &c.*

77. The Lieutenant Governor may from Time to Time, by Instrument under the Great Seal of Quebec, appoint a Member of the Legislative Council of Quebec to be Speaker thereof, and may remove him and appoint another in his stead. *Speaker of Legislative Council.*

78. Until the Legislature of Quebec otherwise provides, the Presence of at least Ten Members of the Legislative Council, including the Speaker, shall be necessary to constitute a Meeting for the Exercise of its Powers. *Quorum of Legislative Council.*

79. Questions arising in the Legislative Council of Quebec shall be decided by a Majority of Voices, and the Speaker shall in all Cases have a Vote, and when the Voices are equal the Decision shall be deemed to be in the negative. *Voting in Legislative Council.*

80. The Legislative Assembly of Quebec shall be composed of Sixty-five Members, to be elected to represent the Sixty-five Electoral Divisions or Districts of Lower Canada in this Act referred to, subject to Alteration thereof by the Legislature of Quebec: Provided that it shall not be lawful to present to the Lieutenant Governor of Quebec for Assent any Bill for altering the Limits of any of the Electoral Divisions or Districts mentioned in the Second Schedule to this Act, unless the Second and Third Readings of such Bill have been passed in the Legislative Assembly with the Concurrence of the Majority of the Members representing all those Electoral Divisions or Districts, and the Assent shall not be given to such Bill unless an Address has been presented by the Legislative Assembly to the Lieutenant Governor stating that it has been so passed. *Constitution of Legislative Assembly of Quebec.*

151

3.—ONTARIO AND QUEBEC.

First Session of Legislatures.

81. The Legislatures of Ontario and Quebec respectively shall be called together not later than Six Months after the Union.

Summoning of Legislative Assemblies.

82. The Lieutenant Governor of Ontario and of Quebec shall from Time to Time, in the Queen's Name, by Instrument under the Great Seal of the Province, summon and call together the Legislative Assembly of the Province.

Restriction of election of holders of offices.

83. Until the Legislature of Ontario or of Quebec otherwise provides, a Person accepting or holding in Ontario or in Quebec any Office, Commission, or Employment, permanent or temporary, at the Nomination of the Lieutenant Governor, to which an annual Salary, or any Fee, Allowance, Emolument, or profit of any Kind or Amount whatever from the Province is attached, shall not be eligible as a Member of the Legislative Assembly of the respective Province, nor shall he sit or vote as such; but nothing in this Section shall make ineligible any Person being a Member of the Executive Council of the respective Province, or holding any of the following Offices, that is to say, the Offices of Attorney General, Secretary and Registrar of the Province, Treasurer of the Province, Commissioner of Crown Lands, and Commissioner of Agriculture and Public Works, and in Quebec Solicitor General, or shall disqualify him to sit or vote in the House for which he is elected provided he is elected while holding such Office.

Continuance of of existing election Laws.

84. Until the Legislatures of Ontario and Quebec respectively otherwise provide, all Laws which at the Union are in force in those Provinces respectively, relative to the following Matters, or any of them, namely,—the Qualifications and Disqualifications of Persons to be elected or to sit or vote as Members of the Assembly of Canada, the Qualifications or Disqualifications of Voters, the Oaths to be taken by Voters, the Returning Officers, their Powers and Duties, the Proceedings at Elections, the Periods during which such Elections may be continued, and the Trial of controverted Elections and the Proceedings incident thereto, the vacating of the Seats of Members and the issuing and Execution of new Writs in case of Seats vacated otherwise than by Dissolution, —shall respectively apply to Elections of Members to serve in the respective Legislative Assemblies of Ontario and Quebec.

Provided that until the Legislature of Ontario otherwise provides, at any Election for a Member of the Legislative Assembly of Ontario for the District of Algoma, in addition to Persons qualified by the Law of the Province of Canada to vote, every male British Subject, aged Twenty-one Years or upwards, being a Householder, shall have a Vote.

Duration of Legislative Assemblies.

85. Every Legislative Assembly of Ontario and every Legislative Assembly of Quebec shall continue for Four Years from the Day of the Return of the Writs for choosing the same (subject nevertheless to either the Legislative Assembly of Ontario or the Legislative Assembly of Quebec being sooner dissolved by the Lieutenant Governor of the Province), and no longer.

Yearly Session of Legislature.

86. There shall be a session of the Legislature of Ontario and of that of Quebec once at least in every Year, so that Twelve Months shall not intervene between the last Sitting of the Legislature in each Province in one Session and its first Sitting in the next Session.

87. The following Provisions of this Act respecting the House of Commons of Canada shall extend and apply to the Legislative Assemblies of Ontario and Quebec, that is to say,— the Provisions relating to the Election of a Speaker originally and on Vacancies, the Duties of the Speaker, the absence of the Speaker, the Quorum, and the Mode of voting, as if those Provisions were here re-enacted and made applicable in Terms to each such Legislative Assembly. *Speaker, Quorum, &c.*

4.—Nova Scotia and New Brunswick.

88. The Constitution of the Legislature of each of the Provinces of Nova Scotia and New Brunswick shall, subject to the Provisions of this Act, continue as it exists at the Union until altered under the Authority of this Act; and the House of Assembly of New Brunswick existing at the passage of this Act shall, unless sooner dissolved, continue for the Period for which it was elected. *Constitutions of the Legislatures of Nova Scotia and New Brunswick.*

5.—Ontario, Quebec, and Nova Scotia.

89. Each of the Lieutenant Governors of Ontario, Quebec and Nova Scotia shall cause Writs to be issued for the First Election of Members of the Legislative Assembly thereof in such Form and by such Person as he thinks fit, and at such Time and addressed to such Returning Officer as the Governor-General directs, and so that the First Election of Member of Assembly for any Electoral District or any Subdivision thereof shall be held at the same Time and at the same Places as the Election for a Member to serve in the House of Commons of Canada for that Electoral District. *First Elections.*

6.—The Four Provinces.

90. The following Provisions of this Act respecting the Parliament of Canada, namely,—the Provisions relating to Appropriation and Tax Bills, the Recommendation of Money Votes, the Assent to Bills, the Disallowance of Acts, and the Signification of Pleasure on Bills reserved,—shall extend and apply to the Legislatures of the several Provinces as if those Provisions were here re-enacted and made applicable in Terms to the respective Provinces and the Legislatures thereof, with the Substitution of the Lieutenant Governor of the Province for the Governor General, of the Governor General for the Queen and for a Secretary of State, of One Year for Two Years, and of the Province for Canada. *Application to Legislatures of provisions respecting money votes, &c.*

VI.—Distribution of Legislative Powers.

Powers of the Parliament.

91. It shall be lawful for the Queen, by and with the Advice and Consent of the Senate and House of Commons, to make Laws for the Peace, Order, and good Government of Canada, in relation to all Matters not coming within the Classes of Subjects by this Act assigned exclusively to the Legislatures of the Provinces; and for greater Certainty, but not so as to restrict the Generality of the foregoing terms of this Section, it is hereby declared that (notwithstanding anything in this Act) the exclusive Legislative Authority of the Parliament *Legislative Authority of Parliament of Canada.*

of Canada extends to all Matters coming within the Classes of Subjects next hereinafter enumerated, that is to say,—

1. The Public Debt and Property.
2. The Regulation of Trade and Commerce.
3. The raising of Money by any Mode or System of Taxation.
4. The borrowing of Money on the Public Credit.
5. Postal Service.
6. The Census and Statistics.
7. Militia, Military and Naval Service, and Defence.
8. The fixing of and providing for the Salaries and Allowances of Civil and other Officers of the Government of Canada.
9. Beacons, Buoys, Lighthouses, and Sable Island.
10. Navigation and Shipping.
11. Quarantine and the Establishment and Maintenance of Marine Hospitals.
12. Sea Coast and Inland Fisheries.
13. Ferries between a Province and any British or Foreign Country or between Two Provinces.
14. Currency and Coinage.
15. Banking, Incorporation of Banks, and the Issue of Paper Money.
16. Savings Banks.
17. Weights and Measures.
18. Bills of Exchange and Promissory Notes.
19. Interest.
20. Legal Tender.
21. Bankruptcy and Insolvency.
22. Patents of Invention and Discovery.
23. Copyrights.
24. Indians, and Lands reserved for the Indians.
25. Naturalization and Aliens.
26. Marriage and Divorce.
27. The Criminal Law, except the Constitution of Courts of Criminal Jurisdiction, but including the Procedure in Criminal Matters.
28. The Establishment, Maintenance, and Management of Penitentiaries.
29. Such Classes of Subjects as are expressly excepted in the Enumeration of the Classes of Subjects by this Act assigned exclusively to the Legislatures of the Provinces.

And any Matter coming within any of the Classes of Subjects enumerated in this Section shall not be deemed to come within the Class of Matters of a local or private Nature comprised in the Enumeration of the Classes of Subjects by this Act assigned exclusively to the Legislatures of the Provinces.

Exclusive Powers of Provincial Legislatures.

Subjects of exclusive Provincial Legislation.

92. In each Province the Legislature may exclusively make Laws in relation to Matters coming within the Classes of Subjects next hereinafter enumerated; that is to say,—

1. The Amendment from Time to Time, notwithstanding anything in this Act, of the Constitution of the Province, except as regards the Office of Lieutenant Governor.
2. Direct Taxation within the Province in order to the Raising of a Revenue for Provincial Purposes.
3. The borrowing of Money on the sole Credit of the Province.
4. The Establishment and Tenure of Provincial Offices and the Appointment and Payment of Provincial Officers.

5. The Management and Sale of the Public Lands belonging to the Province and of the Timber and Wood thereon.
6. The Establishment, Maintenance, and Management of Public and Reformatory Prisons in and for the Province.
7. The Establishment, Maintenance, and· Management of Hospitals, Asylums, Charities, and Eleemosynary Institutions in and for the Province, other than Marine Hospitals.
8. Municipal Institutions in the Province.
9. Shop, Saloon, Tavern, Auctioneer, and other Licenses in order to the raising of a Revenue for Provincial, Local, or Municipal Purposes.
10. Local Works and Undertakings other than such as are of the following Classes:—
    a. Lines of Steam or other Ships, Railways, Canals, Telegraphs, and other Works and Undertakings connecting the Province with any other or others of the Provinces, or extending beyond the Limits of the Province:
    b. Lines of Steam Ships between the Province and any British or Foreign Country:
    c. Such Works as, although wholly situate within the Province, are before or after their Execution declared by tne Parliament of Canada to be for the general Advantage of Canada or for the Advantage of Two or more of the Provinces.
11. The Incorporation of Companies with Provincial Objects.
12. The Solemnization of Marriage in the Province.
13. Property and Civil Rights in the Province.
14. The Administration of Justice in the Province, including the Constitution, Maintenance, and Organization of Provincial Courts, both of Civil and of Criminal Jurisdiction, and including Procedure in Civil Matters in those Courts.
15. The Imposition of Punishment by Fine, Penalty, or Imprisonment for enforcing any Law of the Province made in relation to any Matter coming within any of the Classes of Subjects enumerated in this Section.
16. Generally all Matters of a Merely local or Private Nature in the Province.

Education.

93. In and for each Province the Legislature may exclusively make Laws in relation to Education, subject and according to the following Provisions:— *Legislation respecting Education.*
(1.) Nothing in any such Law shall prejudicially affect any Right or Privilege with respect to Denominational Schools which any Class of Persons have by Law in the Province at the Union:
(2.) All the Powers, Privileges, and Duties at the Union by Law conferred and imposed in Upper Canada on tne Separate Schools and School Trustees of the Queen's Roman Catholic Subjects shall be and the same are hereby extended to the Dissentient Schools of the Queen's Protestant and Roman Catholic Subjects in Quebec:
(3.) Where in any Province a System of Separate or Dissentient Schools exists by Law at the Union or is thereafter established by the Legislature of the Province, an Appeal shall lie to the Governor General in Council from any Act or Decision of any Provincial Authority affecting any Right or Privilege of the Protestant or

Roman Catholic Minority of the Queen's Subjects in relation to Education:

(4.) In case any such Provincial Law as from Time to Time seems to the Governor General in Council requisite for the due Execution of the Provisions of this Section is not made, or in case any Decision of the Governor General in Council on any Appeal under this Section is not duly executed by the proper Provincial Authority in that Behalf, then and in every such Case, and as far only as the Circumstances of each Case require, the Parliament of Canada may make remedial Laws for the due Execution of the Provisions of this Section and of any Decision of the Governor General in Council under this Section.

Uniformity of Laws in Ontario, Nova Scotia, and New Brunswick.

Legislation for uniformity of Laws in three Provinces.

94. Notwithstanding anything in this Act, the Parliament of Canada may make Provision for the Uniformity of all or any of the Laws relative to Property and Civil Rights in Ontario, Nova Scotia, and New Brunswick, and of the Procedure of all or any of the Courts in those Three Provinces, and from and after the passing of any Act in that Behalf the Power of the Parliament of Canada to make Laws in relation to any Matter comprised in any such Act shall, notwithstanding anything in this Act, be unrestricted; but any Act of the Parliament of Canada making Provision for such Uniformity shall not have effect in any Province unless and until it is adopted and enacted as Law by the Legislature thereof.

Agriculture and Immigration.

Concurrent powers of Legislation respecting Agriculture, &c.

95. In each Province the Legislature may make Laws in relation to Agriculture in the Province, and to Immigration into the Province; and it is hereby declared that the Parliament of Canada may from Time to Time make Laws in relation to Agriculture in all or any of the Provinces, and to Immigration into all or any of the Provinces; and any Law of the Legislature of a Province relative to Agriculture or to Immigration shall have effect in and for the Province as long and as far only as it is not repugnant to any Act of the Parliament of Canada.

VII.—JUDICATURE.

Appointment of Judges.

96. The Governor General shall appoint the Judges of the Superior, District, and County Courts in each Province, except those of the Courts of Probate in Nova Scotia and New Brunswick.

Selection of Judges in Ontario, &c.

97. Until the Laws relative to Property and Civil Rights in Ontario, Nova Scotia, and New Brunswick, and the Procedure of the Courts in those Provinces, are made uniform, the Judges of the Courts of those Provinces appointed by the Governor General shall be selected from the respective Bars of those Provinces.

Selection of Judges in Quebec.

98. The Judges of the Courts of Quebec shall be selected from the Bar of that Province.

Tenure of office of Judges of Superior Courts.

99. The Judges of the Superior Courts shall hold office during good Behaviour, but shall be removable by the Governor General on Address of the Senate and House of Commons.

100. The Salaries, Allowances, and Pensions of the Judges Salaries, &c., of the Superior, District, and County Courts (except the Courts of Judges. of Probate in Nova Scotia and New Brunswick), and of the Admiralty Courts in Cases where the Judges thereof are for the Time being paid by Salary, shall be fixed and provided by the Parliament of Canada.

101. The Parliament of Canada may, notwithstanding any- General thing in this Act, from Time to Time, provide for the Con- Court of stitution, Maintenance and Organization of a General Court Appeal, &c. of Appeal for Canada, and for the Establishment of any additional Courts for the better Administration of the Laws of Canada.

VIII.—Revenues; Debts; Assets; Taxation.

102. All Duties and Revenues over which the respective Creation of Legislatures of Canada, Nova Scotia, and New Brunswick Consolidated before and at the Union had and have Power of Appropriation, revenue fund. except such portions thereof as are by this Act reserved to the respective Legislatures of the Provinces, or are raised by them in accordance with the special Powers conferred on them by this Act, shall form One Consolidated Revenue Fund, to be appropriated for the Public Service of Canada in the Manner and subject to the Charges in this Act provided.

103. The Consolidated Revenue Fund of Canada shall be Expenses of permanently charged with the Costs, Charges, and Expenses Collection, &c. incident to the Collection, Management, and Receipt thereof, and the same shall form the first Charge thereon, subject to be reviewed and audited in such Manner as shall be ordered by the Governor General in Council until the Parliament otherwise provides.

104. The annual Interest of the Public Debts of the several Interest of Provinces of Canada, Nova Scotia, and New Brunswick at the Provincial Union shall form the Second Charge on the Consolidated public debts. Revenue Fund of Canada.

105. Unless altered by the Parliament of Canada, the salary Salary of of the Governor General shall be Ten thousand Pounds Sterling Governor Money of the United Kingdom of Great Britain and Ireland, General. payable out of the Consolidated Revenue Fund of Canada, and the same shall form the Third Charge thereon.

106. Subject to the several Payments by this Act charged Appropriation on the Consolidated Revenue Fund of Canada, the same shall from time to be appropriated by the Parliament of Canada for the Public time. Service.

107. All Stocks, Cash, Banker's Balances, and Securities Transfer of for Money belonging to each Province at the time of the Union, stocks, &c. except as in this Act mentioned, shall be the Property of Canada, and shall be taken in Reduction of the amount of the respective Debts of the Provinces at the Union.

108. The Public Works and Property of each Province, Transfer of enumerated in the Third Schedule to this Act, shall be the property in Property of Canada. schedule.

109. All Lands, Mines, Minerals, and Royalties belonging Property in to the several Provinces of Canada, Nova Scotia, and New Lands, Brunswick at the Union, and all Sums then due or payable for Mines, &c. such Lands, Mines, Minerals, or Royalties, shall belong to the several Provinces of Ontario, Quebec, Nova Scotia, and New Brunswick in which the same are situate or arise, subject to any Trusts existing in respect thereof, and to any Interest other than that of the Province in the same.

Assets connected with Provincial debts. •

110. All Assets connected with such Portions of the Public Debt of each Province as are assumed by that Province shall belong to that Province.

Canada to be liable for Provincial debts.

111. Canada shall be liable for the Debts and Liabilities of each Province existing at the Union.

Debts of Ontario and Quebec.

112. Ontario and Quebec conjointly shall be liable to Canada for the amount (if any) by which the Debt of the Province of Canada exceeds at the Union Sixty-two million five hundred thousand dollars, and shall be charged with Interest at the Rate of Five per Centum per Annum thereon.

Assets of Ontario and Quebec.

113. The Assets enumerated in the Fourth Schedule to this Act belonging at the Union to the Province of Canada shall be the Property of Ontario and Quebec conjointly.

Debt of Nova Scotia.

114. Nova Scotia shall be liable to Canada for the Amount (if any) by which its Public Debt exceeds at the Union Eight million dollars, and shall be charged with Interest at the Rate of Five per Centum per Annum thereon.

Debt of New Brunswick.

115. New Brunswick shall be liable to Canada for the Amount (if any) by which its Public Debt exceeds at the Union Seven million Dollars, and shall be charged with Interest at the Rate of Five per Centum per Annum thereon.

Payment of interest to Nova Scotia and New Brunswick.

116. In case the Public Debts of Nova Scotia and New Brunswick do not at the Union amount to Eight million and Seven million Dollars respectively, they shall respectively receive by half-yearly Payments in advance from the Government of Canada Interest at Five per Centum per Annum on the Difference between the actual Amounts of their respective Debts and such stipulated Amounts.

Provincial public property.

117. The several Provinces shall retain all their respective Public Property not otherwise disposed of in this Act, subject to the Right of Canada to assume any Lands or Public Property required for Fortification or for the Defence of the Country.

Grants to Provinces.

118. The following Sums shall be paid yearly by Canada to the several Provinces for the Support of their Governments and Legislatures:

	Dollars.
Ontario	Eighty thousand.
Quebec	Seventy thousand.
Nova Scotia	Sixty thousand.
New Brunswick	Fifty thousand.

Two hundred and sixty thousand;

and an annual Grant in aid of each Province shall be made, equal to Eighty Cents per Head of the Population as ascertained by the Census of One thousand eight hundred and sixty-one, and in the case of Nova Scotia and New Brunswick, by each subsequent Decennial Census until the Population of each of those two Provinces amounts to Four hundred thousand Souls, at which Rate such Grant shall thereafter remain. Such Grants shall be in full Settlement of all future Demands on Canada, and shall be paid half-yearly in advance to each Province; but the Government of Canada shall deduct from such Grants, as against any Province, all Sums chargeable as Interest on the Public Debt of that Province in excess of the several Amounts stipulated in this Act.

119. New Brunswick shall receive by half-yearly Payments in advance from Canada for the Period of Ten years from the Union an additional Allowance of Sixty-three thousand Dollars per Annum; but as long as the Public Debt of that Province remains under Seven million Dollars, a Deduction equal to the Interest at Five per Centum per Annum on such Deficiency shall be made from that Allowance of Sixty-three thousand Dollars. *Further grant to New Brunswick.*

120. All Payments to be made under this Act, or in discharge of Liabilities created under any Act of the Provinces of Canada, Nova Scotia, and New Brunswick respectively, and assumed by Canada, shall, until the Parliament of Canada otherwise directs, be made in such Form and Manner as may from Time to Time be ordered by the Governor General in Council. *Form of payments.*

121. All Articles of the Growth, Produce, or Manufacture of any one of the Provinces shall, from and after the Union, be admitted free into each of the other Provinces. *Canadian manufactures, &c.*

122. The Customs and Excise Laws of each Province shall, subject to the Provisions of this Act, continue in force until altered by the Parliament of Canada. *Continuance of customs and excise laws.*

123. Where Customs Duties are, at the Union, leviable on any Goods, Wares, or Merchandises in any Two Provinces, those Goods, Wares, and Merchandises may, from and after the Union, be imported from one of those Provinces into the other of them on Proof of Payment of the Customs Duty leviable thereon in the Province of Exportation, and on Payment of such further Amount (if any) of Customs Duty as is leviable thereon in the Province of Importation. *Exportation and importation as between two Provinces.*

124. Nothing in this Act shall affect the Right of New Brunswick to levy the Lumber Dues provided in Chapter Fifteen of Title Three of the Revised Statutes of New Brunswick, or in any Act amending that Act before or after the Union, and not increasing the Amount of such Dues; but the Lumber of any of the Provinces other than New Brunswick shall not be subject to such Dues. *Lumber Dues in New Brunswick.*

125. No Lands or Property belonging to Canada or any Province shall be liable to Taxation. *Exemption of Public Lands, &c.*

126. Such Portions of the Duties and Revenues over which the respective Legislatures of Canada, Nova Scotia, and New Brunswick had before the Union Power of Appropriation as are by this Act reserved to the respective Governments or Legislatures of the Provinces, and all Duties and Revenues raised by them in accordance with the special Powers conferred upon them by this Act, shall in each Province form One Consolidated Revenue Fund to be appropriated for the Public Service of the Province. *Provincial Consolidated revenue fund.*

IX.—MISCELLANEOUS PROVISIONS.

General.

As to Legislative Councillors of Provinces becoming senators.

127. If any Person being at the passing of this Act a Member of the Legislative Council of Canada, Nova Scotia, or New Brunswick, to whom a Place in the Senate is offered, does not within Thirty Days thereafter, by Writing under his Hand addressed to the Governor General of the Province of Canada or to the Lieutenant Governor of Nova Scotia or New Brunswick (as the Case may be), accept the same, he shall be deemed to have declined the same; and any Person who, being at the passing of this Act a Member of the Legislative Council of Nova Scotia or New Brunswick, accepts a Place in the Senate shall thereby vacate his Seat in such Legislative Council.

Oath of Allegiance, &c.

128. Every member of the Senate or House of Commons of Canada shall before taking his Seat therein take and subscribe before the Governor General or some Person authorized by him, and every Member of a Legislative Council or Legislative Assembly of any Province shall before taking his Seat therein take and subscribe before the Lieutenant Governor of the Province or some Person authorized by him, the Oath of Allegiance contained in the Fifth Schedule to this Act; and every Member of the Senate of Canada and every Member of the Legislative Council of Quebec shall also, before taking his Seat therein, take and subscribe before the Governor General, or some Person authorized by him, the Declaration of Qualification contained in the same Schedule.

Continuance of existing Laws, Courts, Offices, &c.

129. Except as otherwise provided by this Act, all Laws in force in Canada, Nova Scotia, or New Brunswick at the Union, and all Courts of Civil and Criminal Jurisdiction, and all legal Commissions, Powers, and Authorities, and all Officers, Judicial, Administrative, and Ministerial, existing therein at the Union, shall continue in Ontario, Quebec, Nova Scotia, and New Brunswick respectively, as if the Union had not been made; subject nevertheless (except with respect to such as are enacted by or exist under Acts of the Parliament of Great Britain or of the Parliament of the United Kingdom of Great Britain and Ireland,) to be repealed, abolished, or altered by the Parliament of Canada, or by the Legislature of the respective Province, according to the Authority of the Parliament or of that Legislature under this Act.

Transfer of officers to Canada.

130. Until the Parliament of Canada otherwise provides, all Officers of the several Provinces having Duties to discharge in relation to Matters other than those coming within the Classes of Subjects by this Act assigned exclusively to the Legislatures of the Provinces shall be Officers of Canada, and shall continue to discharge the Duties of their respective Offices under the same Liabilities, Responsibilities, and Penalties as if the Union had not been made.

Appointment of new officers.

131. Until the Parliament of Canada otherwise provides, the Governor General in Council may from Time to Time appoint such Officers as the Governor General in Council deems necessary or proper for the effectual Execution of this Act.

Treaty obligations.

132. The Parliament and Government of Canada shall have all Powers necessary or proper for performing the Obligations of Canada or of any Province thereof, as Part of the British Empire, towards Foreign Countries arising under Treaties between the Empire and such Foreign Countries.

133. Either the English or the French Language may be Use of English used by any Person in the Debates of the Houses of the Par- and French liament of Canada and of the Houses of the Legislature of Languages. Quebec; and both those Languages shall be used in the respective Records and Journals of those Houses; and either of those Languages may be used by any Person or in any Pleading or Process in or issuing from any Court of Canada established under this Act, and in or from all or any of the Courts of Quebec.

The Acts of the Parliament of Canada and of the Legislature of Quebec shall be printed and published in both those Languages.

Ontario and Quebec.

134. Until the Legislature of Ontario or of Quebec other- Appointment wise provides, the Lieutenant Governors of Ontario and Quebec of executive may each appoint under the Great Seal of the Province the officers for following Officers, to hold Office during Pleasure, that is to Ontario and say,—the Attorney General, the Secretary and Registrar of Quebec. the Province, the Treasurer of the Province, the Commissioner of Crown Lands, and the Commissioner of Agriculture and Public Works, and in the Case of Quebec the Solicitor General, and may, by Order of the Lieutenant Governor in Council, from Time to Time prescribe the Duties of those Officers and of the several Departments over which they shall preside or to which they shall belong, and of the Officers and Clerks thereof; and may also appoint other and additional Officers to hold Office during Pleasure, and may from Time to Time prescribe the Duties of those Officers, and of the several Departments over which they shall preside or to which they shall belong, and of the Officers and Clerks thereof.

135. Until the Legislature of Ontario or Quebec otherwise Powers, provides, all Rights, Powers, Duties, Functions, Responsi- duties, &c., bilities, or Authorities at the passing of this Act vested in on of Executive imposed on the Attorney General, Solicitor General, Secretary officers. and Registrar of the Province of Canada, Minister of Finance, Commissioner of Crown Lands, Commissioner of Public Works, and Minister of Agriculture and Receiver General, by any Law, Statute or Ordinance of Upper Canada, Lower Canada, or Canada, and not repugnant to this Act, shall be vested in or imposed on any Officer to be appointed by the Lieutenant Governor for the Discharge of the same or any of them; and the Commissioner of Agriculture and Public Works shall perform the Duties and Functions of the Office of Minister of Agriculture at the passing of this Act imposed by the Law of the Province of Canada, as well as those of the Commissioner of Public Works.

136. Until altered by the Lieutenant Governor in Council, Great Seals. the Great Seals of Ontario and Quebec respectively shall be the same, or of the same Design, as those used in the Provinces of Upper Canada and Lower Canada respectively before their Union as the Province of Canada.

137. The Words "and from thence to the End of the then Construction "next ensuing Session of the Legislature," or Words to the of temporary same Effect, used in any temporary Act of the Province of Acts. Canada not expired before the Union, shall be construed to extend and apply to the next Session of the Parliament of Canada if the subject Matter of the Act is within the Powers of the same, as defined by this Act, or to the next Sessions of the Legislatures of Ontario and Quebec respectively if the Subject Matter of the Act is within the Powers of the same as defined by this Act.

As to errors in names.

138. From and after the Union the Use of the Words "Upper Canada" instead of "Ontario," or "Lower Canada" instead of "Quebec," in any Deed, Writ, Process, Pleading, Document, Matter, or Thing, shall not invalidate the same.

As to issue of Proclamations before Union, to commence after Union.

139. Any Proclamation under the Great Seal of the Province of Canada issued before the Union to take effect at a Time which is subsequent to the Union, whether relating to that Province, or to Upper Canada, or to Lower Canada, and the several Matters and Things therein proclaimed shall be and continue of like Force and Effect as if the Union had not been made.

As to issue of Proclamations after Union.

140. Any Proclamation which is authorized by any Act of the Legislature of the Province of Canada to be issued under the Great Seal of the Province of Canada, whether relating to that Province, or to Upper Canada, or to Lower Canada, and which is not issued before the Union, may be issued by the Lieutenant Governor of Ontario or of Quebec, as its Subject Matter requires, under the Great Seal thereof; and from and after the Issue of such Proclamation the same and the several Matters and Things therein proclaimed shall be and continue of the like Force and Effect in Ontario or Quebec as if the Union had not been made.

Penitentiary.

141. The Penitentiary of the Province of Canada shall, until the Parliament of Canada otherwise provides, be and continue the Penitentiary of Ontario and of Quebec.

Arbitration respecting debts, &c.

142. The Division and Adjustment of the Debts, Credits, Liabilities, Properties, and Assets of Upper Canada and Lower Canada shall be referred to the Arbitrament of Three Arbitrators, One chosen by the Government of Ontario, One by the Government of Quebec, and One by the Government of Canada; and the Selection of the Arbitrators shall not be made until the Parliament of Canada and the Legislatures of Ontario and Quebec have met; and the Arbitrator chosen by the Government of Canada shall not be a Resident either in Ontario or in Quebec.

Division of records.

143. The Governor General in Council may from Time to Time order that such and so many of the Records, Books, and Documents of the Province of Canada as he thinks fit shall be appropriated and delivered either to Ontario or to Quebec, and the same shall thenceforth be the Property of that Province; and any Copy thereof or Extract therefrom, duly certified by the Officer having charge of the Original thereof, shall be admitted as Evidence.

Constitution of townships in Quebec.

144. The Lieutenant Governor of Quebec may from Time to Time, by Proclamation under the Great Seal of the Province, to take effect from a day to be appointed therein, constitute Townships in those Parts of the Province of Quebec in which Townships are not then already constituted, and fix the Metes and Bounds thereof.

X.—Intercolonial Railway.

Duty of Government and Parliament of Canada to make Railway herein described.

145. Inasmuch as the Provinces of Canada, Nova Scotia, and New Brunswick have joined in a Declaration that the Construction of the Intercolonial Railway is essential to the Consolidation of the Union of British North America, and to the Assent thereto of Nova Scotia and New Brunswick, and have consequently agreed that Provision should be made for its immediate Construction by the Government of Canada: Therefore, in order to give effect to that Agreement, it shall be the Duty of the Government and Parliament of Canada to provide for the Commencement within Six Months after the Union, of a Railway connecting the River St. Lawrence with the City of Halifax in Nova Scotia, and for the Construction thereof without Intermission, and the Completion thereof with all practicable Speed.

XI.—Admission of other Colonies.

146. It shall be lawful for the Queen, by and with the Advice of Her Majesty's Most Honourable Privy Council, on Addresses from the Houses of the Parliament of Canada, and from the Houses of the respective Legislatures of the Colonies or Provinces of Newfoundland, Prince Edward Island, and British Columbia, to admit those Colonies or Provinces, or any of them, into the Union, and on Address from the Houses of the Parliament of Canada to admit Rupert's Land and the North-western Territory, or either of them, into the Union, on such Terms and Conditions in each Case as are in the Addresses expressed and as the Queen thinks fit to approve, subject to the Provisions of this Act; and the Provisions of any Order in Council in that behalf shall have effect as if they had been enacted by the Parliament of the United Kingdom of Great Britain and Ireland.

Power to admit Newfoundland, &c., into the Union.

147. In case of the Admission of Newfoundland and Prince Edward Island, or either of them, each shall be entitled to a Representation in the Senate of Canada of Four Members, and (notwithstanding anything in this Act) in case of the Admission of Newfoundland the normal Number of Senators shall be Seventy-six and their maximum Number shall be Eighty-two; but Prince Edward Island when admitted shall be deemed to be comprised in the third of the Three Divisions into which Canada is, in relation to the Constitution of the Senate, divided by this Act, and accordingly, after the Admission of Prince Edward Island, whether Newfoundland is admitted or not, Representation of Nova Scotia and New Brunswick in the Senate shall, as Vacancies occur, be reduced from Twelve to Ten Members respectively, and the Representation of each of those Provinces shall not be increased at any Time beyond Ten, except under the Provisions of this Act for the Appointment of Three or Six additional Senators under the Direction of the Queen.

As to Representation of Newfoundland and Prince Edward Island in Senate.

SCHEDULES.

The FIRST SCHEDULE.

Electoral Districts of Ontario.

A.

Existing Electoral Divisions.

Counties.

1. Prescott.
2. Glengarry.
3. Stormont.
4. Dundas.
5. Russell.

6. Carleton.
7. Prince Edward.
8. Halton.
9. Essex.

RIDINGS OF COUNTIES.

10 North Riding of Lanark.
11. South Riding of Lanark.
12. North Riding of Leeds and North Riding of Grenville.
13. South Riding of Leeds.
14. South Riding of Grenville.
15. East Riding of Northumberland.
16. West Riding of Northumberland (excepting therefrom the Township of South Monaghan).
17. East Riding of Durham.
18. West Riding of Durham.
19. North Riding of Ontario.
20. South Riding of Ontario.
21. East Riding of York.
22. West Riding of York.
23. North Riding of York.
24. North Riding of Wentworth.
25. South Riding of Wentworth.
26. East Riding of Elgin.
27. West Riding of Elgin.
28. North Riding of Waterloo.
29. South Riding of Waterloo.
30. North Riding of Brant.
31. South Riding of Brant.
32. North Riding of Oxford.
33. South Riding of Oxford.
34. East Riding of Middlesex.

CITIES, PARTS OF CITIES, AND TOWNS.

35. West Toronto.
36. East Toronto.
37. Hamilton.
38. Ottawa.
39. Kingston.
40. London.
41. Town of Brockville, with the Township of Elizabethtown thereto attached.
42. Town of Niagara, with the Township of Niagara, thereto attached.
43. Town of Cornwall, with the Township of Cornwall thereto attached.

B.

NEW ELECTORAL DIVISIONS.

44. The Provisional Judicial District of ALGOMA.

The County of BRUCE, divided into Two Ridings, to be called respectively the North and South Ridings:—

45. The North Riding of Bruce to consist of the Townships of Bury, Lindsay, Eastnor, Albermarle, Amabel, Arran, Bruce, Elderslie, and Langeen [Saugeen?], and the Village of Southampton.
46. The South Riding of Bruce to consist of the Townships of Kincardine (including the Village of Kincardine), Greenock, Brant, Huron, Kinross [Kinloss?], Culross, and Carrick.

The County of HURON, divided into Two Ridings, to be called respectively the North and South Ridings:—

47. The North Riding to consist of the Townships of Ashfield, Wawanosh, Turnberry, Howick, Morris, Grey, Colborne, Hullett, including the Village of Clinton, and McKillop.

164

48. The South Riding to consist of the Town of Goderich and the Townships of Goderich, Tuckersmith, Stanley, Hay, Usborne, and Stephen.

The County of MIDDLESEX, divided into Ridings, to be called respectively the North, West, and East Ridings:—

49. The North Riding to consist of the Townships of McGillivray and Biddulph (taken from the County of Huron), and Williams East, Williams West, Adelaide, and Lobo.

50. The West Riding to consist of the Townships of Delaware, Carradoc, Metcalfe, Mosa and Ekfrid, and the Village of Strathroy.

[The East Riding to consist of the Townships now embraced therein, and be bounded as it is at present.]

51. The County of LAMBTON to consist of the Townships of Bosanquet, Warwick, Plympton, Sarnia, Moore, Enniskillen, and Brooke, and the Town of Sarnia.

52. The County of KENT to consist of the Townships of Chatham, Dover, East Tilbury, Romney, Raleigh, and Harwich, and the Town of Chatham.

53. The County of BOTHWELL to consist of the Townships of Sombra, Dawn, and Euphemia (taken from the County of Lambton), and the Townships of Zone, Camden with the Gore thereof, Orford, and Howard (taken from the County of Kent).

The County of GREY, divided into Two Ridings, to be called respectively the South and North Ridings:—

54. The South Riding to consist of the Townships of Bentinck, Glenelg, Artmesia, Osprey, Normanby, Egremont, Proton, and Melancthon.

55. The North Riding to consist of the Townships of Collingwood, Euphrasia, Holland, Saint-Vincent, Sydenham, Sullivan, Derby, and Keppel, Sarawak and Brooke, and the Town of Owen Sound.

The County of PERTH, divided into Two Ridings, to be called respectively the South and North Ridings:—

56. The North Riding to consist of the Townships of Wallace, Elma, Logan, Ellice, Mornington. and North Easthope, and the Town of Stratford.

57. The South Riding to consist of the Townships of Blanchard, Downie, South Easthope, Fullerton, Hibbert, and the Villages of Mitchell and Ste. Mary's.

The County of WELLINGTON, divided into Three Ridings, to be called respectively North, South and Centre Ridings:—

58. The North Riding to consist of the Townships of Amaranth, Arthur, Luther, Minto, Maryborough, Peel, and the Village of Mount Forest.

59. The Centre Riding to consist of the Townships of Garafraxa, Erin, Eramosa, Nichol, and Pilkington, and the Villages of Fergus and Elora.

60. The South Riding to consist of the Town of Guelph, and the Townships of Guelph and Puslinch.

The County of NORFOLK, divided into Two Ridings, to be called respectively the South and North Ridings:—

61. The South Riding to consist of the Townships of Charlotteville, Houghton, Walsingham, and Woodhouse, and with the Gore thereof.

62. The North Riding to consist of the Townships of Middleton, Townsend, and Windham, and the Town of Simcoe.

63. The County of HALDIMAND to consist of the Townships of Oneida, Seneca, Cayuga North, Cayuga South, Rainham, Walpole, and Dunn.

64. The County of MONCK to consist of the Townships of Canborough and Moulton, and Sherbrooke, and the Village of Dunnville (taken from the County of Haldimand), the Townships of Caister and Gainsborough (taken from the County of Lincoln), and the Townships of Pelham and Wainfleet (taken from the County of Welland).

65. The County of LINCOLN to consist of the Townships of Clinton, Grantham, Grimsby, and Louth, and the Town of St. Catherines.

66. The County of WELLAND to consist of the Townships of Bertie, Crowland, Humberstone, Stamford, Thorold, and Willoughby, and the Villages of Chippewa, Clifton, Fort Erie, Thorold, and Welland.

67. The County of PEEL to consist of the Townships of Chinguacousy, Toronto, and the Gore of Toronto, and the Villages of Brampton and Streetsville.

68. The County of CARDWELL to consist of the Townships of Albion and Caledon (taken from the County of Peel), and the Townships of Adjala and Mono (taken from the County of Simcoe).

The County of SIMCOE, divided into two Ridings, to be called respectively the South and North Ridings:—

69. The South Riding to consist of the Townships of West Gwillimbury, Tecumseth, Innisfil, Essa, Tossorontio, Mulmur, and the Village of Bradford.

70. The North Riding to consist of the Townships of Nottawasaga, Sunnidale, Vespra, Flos, Oro, Medonte, Orillia and Matchedash, Tiny and Tay, Balaklava and Robinson, and the Towns of Barrie and Collingwood.

The County of VICTORIA, divided into Two Ridings, to be called respectively the South and North Ridings:—

71. The South Riding to consist of the Townships of Ops, Mariposa, Emily, Verulam, and the Town of Lindsay.

72. The North Riding to consist of the Townships of Anson, Bexley, Carden, Dalton, Digby, Eldon, Fenelon, Hindon, Laxton, Lutterworth, Macaulay and Draper, Sommerville, and Morrison, Muskoka, Monck and Watt (taken from the County of Simcoe), and any other surveyed Townships lying to the North of the said North Riding.

The County of PETERBOROUGH, divided into Two Ridings, to be called respectively the West and East Ridings:—

73. The West Riding to consist of the Townships of South Monaghan (taken from the County of Northumberland), North Monaghan, Smith, and Ennismore, and the Town of Peterborough.

74. The East Riding to consist of the Townships of Asphodel, Belmont and Methuen, Douro, Dummer, Galway, Harvey, Minden, Stanhope and Dysart, Otonabee, and Snowden, and the Village of Ashburnham, and any other surveyed Townships lying to the North of the said East Riding.

The County of HASTINGS, divided into Three Ridings, to be called respectively the West, East and North Ridings:—

75. The West Riding to consist of the Town of Belleville, the Township of Sydney, and the Village of Trenton.

76. The East Riding to consist of the Townships of Thurlow, Tyendinaga, and Hungerford.

77. The North Riding to consist of the Townships of Rawdon, Huntingdon, Madoc, Elzevir, Tudor, Marmora, and Lake and the Village of Stirling and any other surveyed Townships lying to the North of the said North Riding.

78. The County of LENNOX, to consist of the Townships of Richmond, Adolphustown, North Fredericksburgh, South Fredericksburgh, Ernest Town and Amherst Island, and the Village of Napanee.

79. The County of ADDINGTON to consist of the Townships of Camden, Portland, Sheffield, Hinchinbrooke, Kaladar, Kennebec, Olden, Oso, Anglesea, Barrie, Clarendon, Palmerston, Effingham, Abinger, Miller, Canonto, Denbigh, Loughborough, and Bedford.

80. The County of FRONTENAC to consist of the Townships of Kingston, Wolfe Island, Pittsburg, and Howe Island, and Storrington.

The County of RENFREW, divided into two Ridings, to be called respectively the South and North Ridings:—

81. The South Riding to consist of the Townships of McNab, Bagot, Blithfield, Brougham, Horton, Admaston, Grattan, Matawatchan, Griffith, Lyndoch. Raglan, Radcliffe, Brudenell, Sebastapol, and the Villages of Arnprior and Renfrew.

82. The North Riding to consist of the Townships of Ross, Bromley, Westmeath, Stafford, Pembroke, Wilberforce, Alice, Petewawa, Buchanan, South Algona, North Algona, Fraser, McKay, Wylie, Rolph, Head, Maria, Clara, Haggerty, Sherwood, Burns, and Richards, and any other surveyed Townships lying North-westerly of the said North Riding.

———

Every Town and incorporated Village existing at the Union, not specially mentioned in this Schedule, is to be taken as Part of the County or Riding within which it is locally situate.

The SECOND SCHEDULE.

Electoral Districts of Quebec specially fixed.

COUNTIES OF—

Pontiac.	Missisquoi.	Compton.
Ottawa.	Brome.	Wolfe and Richmond.
Argenteuil.	Shefford.	Megantic.
Huntingdon.	Stanstead.	
	Town of Sherbrooke.	

The THIRD SCHEDULE.

Provincial Public Works and Property to be the Property of Canada.

1. Canals, with Lands and Water Power connected therewith.
2. Public Harbours.
3. Lighthouses and Piers, and Sable Island.
4. Steamboats, Dredges, and Public Vessels.
5. Rivers and Lake Improvement.
6. Railways and Railway Stocks, Mortgages, and other Debts due by Railway Companies.
7. Military Roads.
8. Custom Houses, Post Offices, and all other Public Buildings, except such as the Government of Canada appropriate for the Use of the Provincial Legislatures and Governments.
9. Property transferred by the Imperial Government, and known as Ordnance Property.
10. Armouries, Drill Sheds, Military Clothing, and Munitions of War, and Lands set apart for general Public Purposes.

The FOURTH SCHEDULE.

Assets to be the Property of Ontario and Quebec conjointly.

Upper Canada Building Fund.
Lunatic Asylums.
Normal School.
Court Houses
in
Aylmer,   } Lower Canada.
Montreal,
Kamouraska,
Law Society, Upper Canada.
Montreal Turnpike Trust.
University Permanent Fund.
Royal Institution.
Consolidated Municipal Loan Fund, Upper Canada.
Consolidated Municipal Loan Fund, Lower Canada.
Agricultural Society, Upper Canada.
Lower Canada Legislative Grant.
Quebec Fire Loan.
Temisconata [Temiscouata?] Advance Account.
Quebec Turnpike Trust.
Education—East.
Building and Jury Fund, Lower Canada.
Municipalities Fund.
Lower Canada Superior Education Income Fund.

The FIFTH SCHEDULE.

OATH OF ALLEGIANCE.

I, *A. B.*, do swear, That I will be faithful and bear true Allegiance to Her Majesty Queen Victoria.

Note.—The Name of the King or Queen of the United Kingdom of Great Britain and Ireland for the Time being is to be substituted from Time to Time, with Proper Terms of Reference thereto.

DECLARATION OF QUALIFICATION.

I, *A. B.*, do declare and testify, That I am by Law duly qualified to be appointed a Member of the Senate of Canada [*or as the Case may be*], and that I am legally or equitably seised as of Freehold for my own Use and Benefit of Lands or Tenements held in Free and Common Socage [*or seised or possessed for my own Use and Benefit of Lands or Tenements held in Franc-alleu or in Roture (as the Case may be*),] in the Province of Nova Scotia [*or as the Case may be*] of the Value of Four Thousand Dollars over and above all Rents, Dues, Debts, Mortgages, Charges, and Incumbrances due or payable out of or charged on or affecting the same, and that I have not collusively or colourably obtained a Title to or become possessed of the said Lands and Tenements or any Part thereof for the Purpose of enabling me to become a Member of the Senate of Canada [*or as the Case may be*], and that my Real and Personal Property are together worth Four Thousand Dollars over and above my Debts and Liabilities.

F. A. Acland, Printer to the King's Most Excellent Majesty, Ottawa, Canada